The House in the Water

by Charles G. D. Roberts

CONTENTS OF THE BOOK

THE HOUSE IN THE WATER

CHAPTER I

The Sound in the Night

UPON the moonlit stillness came suddenly a far-off, muffled, crashing sound. Just once it came, then once again the stillness of the wilderness night, the stillness of vast, untraversed solitude. The Boy lifted his eyes and glanced across the thin reek of the camp-fire at Jabe Smith, who sat smoking contemplatively. Answering the glance, the woodsman muttered "old tree fallin'," and resumed his passive contemplation of the sticks glowing keenly in the fire. The Boy, upon whom, as soon as he entered the wilderness, the taciturnity of the woodsfolk descended as a garment, said nothing, but scanned his companion's gaunt face with a gravely incredulous smile.

So wide-spread and supreme was the silence that five seconds after that single strange sound had died out it seemed, somehow, impossible to believe it had ever been. The light gurgle of the shallow and shrunken brook which ran past the open front of the travellers' "lean-to" served only to measure the stillness. Both Jabe and the Boy, since eating their dinner, had gradually forgotten to talk. As the moon rose over the low, fir-crested hills they had sunk into reverie, watching the camp-fire die down.

At last, with a sort of crisp whisper a stick, burnt through the middle, fell apart, and a flicker of red flame leaped up. The woodsman knocked out his pipe, rose slowly to his feet, stretched his gaunt length, and murmured,

"Reckon we might as well turn in."

"That's all right for you, Jabe," answered the Boy, rising also, tightening his belt, and reaching for his rifle, "but I'm going off to see what I can see. Night's the time to see things in the woods."

Jabe grunted non-committally, and began spreading his blanket in the lean-to. "Don't forgit to come back for breakfast, that's all," he muttered. He regarded the Boy as a phenomenally brilliant hunter and trapper spoiled by sentimental notions.

To the Boy, whose interest in all pertaining to woodcraft was much broader and more sympathetic than that of his companion, Jabe's interpretation of the sound of the falling tree had seemed hasty and shallow. He knew that there was no better all-round woodsman in these countries than Jabe Smith; but he knew also that Jabe's interest in the craft was limited pretty strictly to his activities as hunter, trapper and lumberman. Just now he was all lumberman. He was acting as what is called a "timber-cruiser," roaming the remoter and less-known regions of the wilderness to locate the best growths of spruce and pine for the winter's lumbering operations, and for the present his keen faculties were set on the noting of tree growths, and water-courses, and the lay of the land for the getting out of a winter's cutting. On this particular cruise the Boy--who, for all the disparity in their years and the divergence in their views, was his most valued comrade--had accompanied him with a special object in view. The region they were cruising was one which had never been adequately explored, and it was said to be full of little unnamed, unmapped lakes and streams, where, in former days, the Indians had had great beaver hunting.

When the sound of the falling tree came to his ears across the night-silence, the Boy at once said to himself, "Beavers, at work!" He said it to himself, not aloud, because he knew that Jabe also, as a trapper, would be interested in beavers; and he had it in his mind to score a point on Jabe. Noiseless as a lynx in his soft-soled "larrigans," he ascended the half-empty channel of the brook, which here strained its shrunken current through rocks and slate-slabs, between steep banks. The channel curved steadily, rounding the shoulder of a low ridge. When he felt that he had travelled somewhat less than half a mile, he came out upon a bit of swampy marsh, beyond which, over the crest of a low dam, spread the waters of a tranquil pond shining like a mirror in the moonlight.

The Boy stopped short, his heart thumping with excitement and anticipation. Here before him was what he had come so far to find. From his books and from his innumerable talks with hunter and trapper, he knew that the dam and the shining, lonely pond were the work of beavers. Presently he distinguished amid the sheen of the water a tiny, grassy islet, with a low, dome-shaped, stick-covered mound at one end of it. This, plainly, was a beaver house, the first he had ever seen. His delighted eyes, observing it at this distance, at once pronounced it immeasurably superior to the finest and most pretentious muskrat-house he had ever seen--a very palace, indeed, by comparison. Then, a little further up the pond, and apparently adjoining the shore, he made out another dome-shaped structure, broader and less conspicuous than the first, and more like a mere pile of sticks. The pond, which was several acres in extent, seemed to him an extremely spacious domain for the dwellers in these two houses.

Presently he marked a black trail, as it were, moving down in the middle of the radiance from the upper end of the pond. It was obviously the trail of some swimmer, but much too broad, it seemed, to be made by anything so small as a beaver. It puzzled him greatly. In his eagerness he pushed noiselessly forward, seeking a better view, till he was within some thirty feet of the dam. Then he made out a small dark spot in the front of the trail,-- evidently a beaver's head; and at last he detected that the little swimmer was carrying a bushy branch, one end held in his mouth while the rest was slung back diagonally across his shoulders.

The Boy crept forward like a cat, his gray eyes shining with expectancy. His purpose was to gain a point where he could crouch in ambush behind the dam, and perhaps get a view of the lake-dwellers actually at work. He was within six or eight feet of the dam, crouching low (for the dam was not more than three feet in height), when his trained and cunning ear caught a soft swirling sound in the water on the other side of the barrier. Instantly he stiffened to a statue, just as he was, his mouth open so that not a pant of his quickened breath might be audible. The next moment the head of a beaver appeared over the edge of the dam, not ten feet away, and stared him straight in the face.

The beaver had a stick of alder in its mouth, to be used, no doubt, in some repairing of the dam. The Boy, all in gray as he was, and absolutely motionless, trusted to be mistaken for one of the gnarled, gray stumps with which the open space below the dam was studded. He had read that the beaver was very near-sighted, and on that he based his hopes, though he was so near, and the moonlight so clear, that he could see the bright eyes of the newcomer staring straight into his with insistent question. Evidently, the story of that near-sightedness had not been exaggerated. He saw the doubt in the beaver's eye fade gradually into confidence, as the little animal became convinced that the strange gray figure was in reality just one of the stumps. Then, the industrious dam-builder began to climb out upon the crest of the dam, dragging his huge and hairless tail, and glancing along as if to determine where the stick which he carried would do most good. At this critical moment, when the eager watcher felt that he was just about to learn the exact methods of these wonderful architects of the wild, a stick in the slowly settling mud beneath his feet broke with a soft, thick-muffled snap.

So soft was the sound that it barely reached the Boy's ears. To the marvellously sensitive ears of the beaver, however, it was a warning more than sufficient. It was a noisy proclamation of peril. Swift as a wink of light, the beaver dropped his stick and dived head first into the pond. The Boy straightened up just in time to see him vanish. As he vanished, his broad, flat, naked tail hit the water with a cracking slap which resounded over the pond like a pistol-shot. It was re-echoed by four or five more splashes from the upper portion of the pond. Then all was silence again, and the Boy realized that there would be no more chance that night for him to watch the little people of the House in the Water. Mounting the firm-woven face of the dam and casting his eyes all over the pond, he satisfied himself that two houses which he had first seen were all that it contained. Then, resisting the impulse of his excitement, which was to explore all around the pond's borders at once, he resolutely turned his face back to camp, full of thrilling plans for the morrow.

CHAPTER II

The Battle in the Pond

AT breakfast, in the crisp of the morning, while yet the faint mists clung over the brook and the warmth of the camp-fire was attractive, the Boy proclaimed his find. Jabe had asked no questions, inquisitiveness being contrary to the backwoodsman's code of etiquette; but his silence had been full of interrogation. With his mouth half-full of fried trout and cornbread, the Boy remarked:

"That was no windfall, Jabe, that noise we heard last night!"

"So?" muttered the woodsman, rather indifferently.

Without a greater show of interest than that the Boy would not divulge his secret. He helped himself to another flaky pink section of trout, and became seemingly engrossed in it. Presently the woodsman spoke again. He had been thinking, and had realized that his prestige had suffered some kind of blow.

"Of course," drawled the woodsman sarcastically, "it wa'n't no windfall. I jest said that to git quit of bein' asked questions when I was sleepy. I knowed all the time it was beaver!"

"Yes, Jabe," admitted the Boy, "it was beavers. I've found a big beaver-pond just up the brook a ways--a pond with two big beaver-houses in it. I've found it--so I claim it as mine, and there ain't to be any trapping on that pond. Those are my beavers, Jabe, every one of them, and they sha'n't be shot or trapped!"

"I don't know how fur yer injunction'd hold in law," said Jabe dryly, as he speared a thick slab of bacon from the frying-pan to his tin plate. "But fur as I'm concerned, it'll hold. An' I reckon the boys of the camp this winter'll respect it, too, when I tell 'em as how it's your own partic'lar beaver pond."

"Bless your old heart, Jabe!" said the Boy. "That's just what I was hoping. And I imagine anyway there's lots more beaver round this region to be food for the jaws of your beastly old traps!"

"Yes," acknowledged Jabe, rising to clear up, "I struck three likely ponds yesterday, as I was cruisin over to west'ard of the camp. I reckon we kin spare you the sixteen or twenty beaver in 'Boy's Pond!'"

The Boy grinned appreciation of the notable honour done him in the naming of the pond, and a little flush of pleasure deepened the red of his cheeks. He knew that the name would stick, and eventually go upon the maps, the lumbermen being a people tenacious of tradition and not to be swerved from their own way.

"Thank you, Jabe!" he said simply. "But how do you know there are sixteen or twenty beaver in my pond?"

"You said there was two houses," answered the woodsman. "Well, we reckon always from eight to ten beaver to each house, bein' the old couple, and then three or four yearlin's not yet kicked out to set up housekeeping fer themselves, and three or four youngsters of the spring's whelping. Beavers' good parents, an' the family holds together long's the youngsters needs it. Now I'm off. See you here at noon, fer grub!" and picking up his axe he strode off to southwestward of the camp to investigate a valley which he had located the day before.

Left alone, the Boy hurriedly set the camp in order, rolled up the blankets, washed the dishes, and put out the last of the fire. Then, picking up his little Winchester, which he always carried,--though he never used it on anything more sensitive than a bottle or a tin can,--he retraced his steps of the night before, up-stream to the beaver pond.

Knowing that the beavers do most of their work, or, at least, most of their above-water work, at night, he had little hope of catching any of them abroad by daylight. He approached the dam, nevertheless, with that noiseless caution which had become a habit with him in the woods, a habit which rendered the woods populous for him and teeming with interest, while to more noisy travellers they seemed quite empty of life. One thing his study of the wilderness had well taught him, which was that the wild kindreds do not by any means always do just what is expected of them, but rather seem to delight in contradicting the naturalists.

When he reached the edge of the open, however, and peered out across the dam, there was absolutely nothing to break the shining morning stillness. In the clear sunlight the dam, and the two beaver-houses beyond, looked larger and more impressive than they had looked the night before. There was no sign of life anywhere about the pond, except a foraging fish-hawk winging above it, with fierce head stretched low in the search for some basking trout or chub.

Following the usual custom of the wild kindreds themselves, the Boy stood motionless for some minutes behind his thin screen of bushes before revealing himself frankly in the open. His patient watch being unrewarded, he was on the very verge of stepping forth, when from the tail of his eye he caught a motion in the shallow bed of the brook, and ducked himself. He was too wary to turn his head; but a moment later a little brown sinuous shape came into his field of view. It was an otter, making his way up-stream.

The otter moved with unusual caution, glancing this way and that and seeming to take minute note of all he saw. At the foot of the dam he stopped, and investigated the structure with the air of one who had never seen it before. So marked was this air that the Boy concluded he was a stranger to that region,--perhaps a wanderer from the head of the Ottanoonsis, some fifteen miles southward, driven away by the operations of a crew of lumbermen who were building a big lumber-camp there. However that might be, it was evident that the brown traveller was a newcomer, an outsider. He had none of the confident, businesslike manner which a wild animal wears in moving about his own range.

When he had stolen softly along the whole base of the dam, and back again, nosing each little rivulet of overflow, the otter seemed satisfied that this was much like all other beaver dams. Then he mounted to the crest and took a prolonged survey of the stretch of water beyond. Nothing unusual appearing, he dived cleanly into the pond, about the point where, as the Boy guessed, there would be the greatest depth of water against the dam. He was apparently heading straight up for the inlet of the pond, on a path which would take him within about twenty-five or thirty yards of the main beaver-house on the island. As soon as he had vanished under the water the Boy ran forward, mounted the crest of the dam, and peered with shaded eyes to see if he could mark the swimmer's progress.

For a couple of minutes, perhaps, the surface of the pond gave no indication of the otter's whereabouts. Then, just opposite the main beaver-house, there was a commotion in the water, the surface curled and eddied, and the otter appeared in great excitement. He dived again immediately; and just as he did so the head of a huge beaver poked up and snatched a breath. Where the two had gone under, the surface of the pond now fairly boiled; and the Boy, in his excitement over this novel and mysterious contest, nearly lost his balance on the frail crest of the dam. A few moments more and both adversaries again came to the surface, now at close grips and fighting furiously. They were followed almost at once by a second beaver, smaller than the first, who fell upon the otter with insane fury. It was plain that the beavers were the aggressors. The Boy's sympathies were all with the otter, who from time to time tried vainly to escape from the battle; and once he raised his rifle. But he bethought him that the otter, after all, whatever his intentions, was a trespasser; and that the beavers had surely a right to police their own pond. He remembered an old Indian's having told him that there was always a blood feud between the beaver and the otter; and how was he to know how just the cause of offence, or the stake at issue? Lowering his gun he stared in breathless eagerness.

The otter, however, as it proved, was well able to take care of himself. Suddenly rearing his sleek, snaky body half out of the water, he flashed down upon the smaller beaver and caught it firmly behind the ear with his long, deadly teeth--teeth designed to hold the convulsive and slippery writhings of the largest salmon. With mad contortions the beaver struggled to break that fatal grip. But the otter held inexorably, shaking its victim as a terrier does a rat, and paid no heed whatever to the slashing assaults of the other beaver. The water was lashed to such a turmoil that the waves spread all over the pond, washing up to the Boy's feet on the crest of the dam, and swaying the bronze-green grasses about the house on the little island. Though, without a doubt, all the other citizens of the pond were watching the battle even more intently than himself, the Boy could not catch sight of so much as nose or ear. The rest of the spectators kept close to the covert of grass tuft and lily pad.

All at once the small beaver stiffened itself out convulsively on top of the water, turned belly up, and began to sink. At the same time the otter let go, tore free of his second and more dangerous adversary, and swam desperately for the nearest point of shore. The surviving beaver, evidently hurt, made no effort to follow up his victory, but paddled slowly to the house on the island, where he disappeared. Presently the otter gained the shore and dragged himself up. His glossy brown skin was gashed and streaming with blood, but the Boy gathered that his wounds were not mortal. He turned, stared fixedly at the beaver-house for several seconds as if unwilling to give in, then stole off through the trees to seek some more hospitable water. As he vanished, repulsed and maltreated, the Boy realized for the first time how hostile even the unsophisticated wilderness is to a stranger. Among the wild kindreds, even as among men, most things worth having are preempted.

When the Boy's excitement over this strange fight had calmed down, he set himself with keen interest to examining the dam. He knew that by this time every beaver in the pond was aware of his presence, and would take good care to keep out of sight; so there was no longer anything to be gained by concealment. Pacing the crest, he made it to be about one hundred feet in length. At the centre, and through a great part of its length, it was a little over three feet high, its ends diminishing gradually into the natural rise of the shores. The base of the dam, as far as he could judge, seemed to be about twelve feet in thickness, its upper face constructed with a much more gradual slope than the lower. The whole structure, which was built of poles, brush, stones, and earth, appeared to be very substantial, a most sound and enduring piece of workmanship. But along the crest, which was not more than a foot and a half in width, it was built with a certain looseness and elasticity for which he was at a loss to account. Presently he observed, however, that this dam had no place of overflow for letting off the water. The water stood in the pond at a height that brought it within three or four inches of the crest. At this level he saw that it was escaping, without violence, by percolating through the toughly but loosely woven tissue of sticks and twigs. The force of the overflow was thus spread out so thin that its destructive effect on the dam was almost nothing. It went filtering, with little trickling noises, down over and through the whole lower face of the structure, there to gather again into a brook and resume its sparkling journey toward the sea.

The long upper slope of the dam was smoothly and thoroughly faced with clay, so that none of its framework showed through, save here and there the butt of a sapling perhaps three or four inches in diameter, which proclaimed the solidity of the foundations. The lower face, on the other hand, was all an inexplicable interlacing of sticks and poles which seemed at first glance heaped together at haphazard. On examination, however, the Boy found that every piece was woven in so firmly among its fellows that it took some effort to remove it. The more he studied the structure, the more his admiration grew, and his appreciation of the reasoning intelligence of its builders; and he smiled to himself a little controversial smile, as he thought how inadequate what men call instinct would be to such a piece of work as this.

But what impressed him most, as a mark of engineering skill and sound calculation on the part of the pond-people, was the direction in which the dam was laid. At either end, where the water was shoal, and comparatively dead even in time of freshet, the dam ran straight, taking the shortest way. But where it crossed the main channel of the brook, and required the greatest strength, it had a pronounced upward curve to help it resist the thrust of the current. He contemplated this strong curve for some time; then, a glance at the sun reminding him that it was near noon, he took off his cap to the low-domed house in the water and made haste back to camp for dinner.

CHAPTER III

In the Under-water World

MEANWHILE, in the dark chamber and the long, dim corridors of the House in the Water there was great perturbation. The battle with the otter had been a tremendous episode in their industrious, well-ordered lives, and they were wildly excited over it. But much more important to them--to all but the big beaver who was now nursing his triumphant wounds--was the presence of Man in their solitude. Man had hitherto been but a tradition among them, a vague but alarming tradition. And now his appearance, yesterday and to-day, filled them with terror. That vision of the Boy, standing tall and ominous on the dam, and afterwards going forward and backward over it, pulling at it, apparently seeking to destroy it, seemed to portend mysterious disasters. After he was gone, and well gone, almost every beaver in the pond, not only from the main house but also from the lodge over on the bank, swam down and made a flurried inspection of the dam, without showing his head above water, to see if the structure on which they all depended had been tampered with. One by one, each on his own responsibility, they swam down and inspected the water-face; and one by one they swam back, more or less relieved in their minds.

All, of course, except the big beaver who had been in the fight. If it had not been for that vision of the Boy, he would have crept out upon the dry grass of the little island and there licked and comforted his wounds in the comforting sunlight. Now, however, he dared not allow himself that luxury. His strong love of cleanliness made him reluctant to take his bleeding gashes into the house; but there was nothing else to be done. He was the head of the household, however, so there was none to gainsay him. He dived into the mouth of the shorter of the two entrances, mounted the crooked and somewhat steep passage, and curled himself upon the dry grass in one corner of the dark, secluded chamber. His hurts were painful, and ugly, but none of them deadly, and he knew he would soon be all right again. There was none of that foreknowledge of death upon him which sometimes drives a sick animal to abdicate his rights and crawl away by himself for the last great contest.

The room wherein the big beaver lay down to recover himself was not spacious nor particularly well ventilated, but in every other respect it was very admirably adapted to the needs of its occupants. Through the somewhat porous ceiling, a three-foot thickness of turf and sticks, came a little air, but no light. This, however, did not matter to the beavers, whose ears and noses were of more significance to them than their eyes. In floor area the chamber was something like five feet by six and a half, but in height not much more than eighteen inches. The floor of this snug retreat was not five inches above the level of the water in the passages leading in to it; but so excellently was it constructed as to be altogether free from damp. It was daintily clean, moreover; and the beds of dry grass around the edges of the chamber were clean and fresh.

From this room the living, sleeping, and dining room of the beaver family, ran two passageways communicating with the outside world. Both of these were roofed over to a point well outside the walls of the house, and had their opening in the bottom of the pond, where the water was considerably more than three feet in depth. One of these passages was perfectly straight, about two feet in width, and built on a long, gradual slope. It was by this entrance that the house-dwellers were wont to bring in their food supplies, in the shape of sticks of green willow, birch and poplar. When these sticks were stripped clean of their bark, which was the beavers' chief nourishment, they were then dragged out again, and floated down to be used in the repair of the dam. The other passage, especially adapted to quick exit in case of danger from the way of the roof, was about as spacious as the first, but much shorter and steeper. It was crooked, moreover,--for a reason doubtless adequate to the architects, but obscure to mere human observers. The exits of both passages were always in open water, no matter how fierce the frosts of the winter, how thick the armour of ice over the surface of the pond. In the neighbourhood of the house were springs bubbling up through the bottom, and keeping the temperature of the pond fairly uniform throughout the coldest weather, so that the ice, at worst, never attained a thickness of more than a foot and a half, even though in the bigger lakes of that region it might make to a depth of three feet and over.

While the wounded beaver lay in the chamber licking his honourable gashes, two other members of the family entered and approached him. In some simple but adequate speech it was conveyed to them that their presence was not required, and they retreated precipitately, taking different exits. One swam to the grassy edge of the islet, poked his head above water under the covert of some drooping weeds, listened motionless for some minutes, then wormed himself out among the long grasses and lay basking, hidden from all the world but the whirling hawk overhead. The other, of a more industrious mould, swam off toward the upper end of the pond where, as he knew, there was work to be done.

Still as was the surface of the pond, below the surface there was life and movement. Every little while the surface would be softly broken, and a tiny ripple would set out in widening circles toward the shore, starting from a small dark nose thrust up for a second. The casual observer would have said that these were fish rising for flies; but in fact it was the apprehensive beavers coming up to breathe, afraid to show themselves on account of the Boy. They were all sure that he had not really gone, but was in hiding somewhere, waiting to pounce upon them.

It was the inhabitants of the House in the Water who were moving about the pond, this retreat being occupied by their wounded and ill-humoured champion. The inhabitants of the other house, over on the shore, who had been interested but remote spectators through all the strange events of the morning, were now in comfortable seclusion, resting till it should be counted a safe time to go about their affairs. Some were sleeping, or gnawing on sappy willow sticks, in the spacious chamber of their house, while others were in the deeper and more secret retreats of their two burrows high up in the bank, connecting with the main house by roomy tunnels partly filled with water. The two families were quite independent of each other, except for their common interest in keeping the great dam in repair. In work upon the dam they acted not exactly in harmony but in amicable rivalry, all being watchful and all industrious.

In the under-water world of the beaver pond the light from the cloudless autumn sun was tawny gold, now still as crystal, now quivering over the bottom in sudden dancing meshes of fine shadow as some faint puff of air wrinkled the surface. When the dam was first built the pond had been of proper depth--from three to four feet--only in the channel of the stream; while all the rest was shallow, the old, marshy levels of the shore submerged to a depth of perhaps not more than twelve or fifteen inches. Gradually, however, the industrious dam-builders had dug away these shallows, using the material--grass, roots, clay, and stones--for the broadening and solidifying of the dam. The tough fibred masses of grass-roots, full of clay and almost indestructible, were just such material as they loved to work with, the ancient difficulty of making bricks without straw being well known to them. Over a large portion of the pond the bottom was now clean sand and mud, offering no obstacle to the transportation of cuttings to the houses or the dam.

The beavers, moving hither and thither through this glimmering golden underworld, swam with their powerful hind feet only, which drove them through the water like wedges. Their little forefeet, with flexible, almost handlike paws, were carried tucked up snugly under their chins, while their huge, broad, flat, hairless tails stuck straight out behind, ready to be used as a powerful screw in case of any sudden need. Presently two of the swimmers, apparently by chance, came upon the body of the beaver which the journeying otter had slain. They knew that it was contrary to the laws of the clan that any dead thing should be left in the pond to poison the waters in its decay. Without ceremony or sentiment they proceeded to drag their late comrade toward shore,--or rather to shove it ahead of them, only dragging when it got stuck against some stone or root. At the very edge of the pond, where the water was not more than eight or ten inches deep, they left it, to be thrust out and far up the bank after nightfall. They knew that some hungry night prowler would then take care of it for them.

Meanwhile an industriously inclined beaver had made his way to the very head of the pond. Here he entered a little ditch or canal which led off through a wild meadow in a perfectly straight line, toward a wooded slope some fifty yards or so from the pond. This ditch, which was perhaps two feet and a half deep and about the same in width, looked as if it had been dug by the hand of man. The materials taken from it had been thrown up along the brink, but not on one side only, as the human ditch-digger does it. The beavers had thrown it out on both sides. The ditch was of some age, however, so the wild grasses and weeds had completely covered the two parallel ridges and now leaned low over the water, partly hiding it. Under this screen the beaver came to the surface, and swam noiselessly with his head well up.

At the edge of the slope the canal turned sharply to the left, and ran in a gradual curve, skirting the upland. Here it was a piece of new work, raw and muddy, and the little ridges of fresh earth and roots along its brink were conspicuous. The beaver now went very cautiously, sniffing the air for any hint of peril. After winding along for some twenty or thirty yards, the new canal shoaled out to nothingness behind a screen of alder; and here, in a mess of mud and water, the beaver found one of his comrades hard at work.

There was much of the new canal yet to do, and winter coming on.

The object of this new ditch was to tap a new food supply. The food trees near enough to the pond to be felled into it or rolled down to it had long ago been used. Then the straight canal across the meadow to the foot of the upland had opened up a new area, an area rich in birch and poplar. But trees can be rolled easily down-hill that cannot be dragged along an uneven side-hill; so, at last, it had become necessary to extend the canal parallel with the bottom of the slope. Working in this direction, every foot of new ditch brought a lot of new supplies within reach.

The extremity of the canal was dug on a slant, for greater ease in removing the material. Here the two beavers toiled side by side, working independently. With their teeth they cut the tough sod as cleanly as a digger's spade could do it. With their fore paws they scraped up the soil--which was soft and easily worked--into sticky lumps, which they could hug under their chins and carry up the slope to be dumped upon the grass at the side. Every minute one or the other would stop, lift his brown head over the edge, peer about, and sniff, and listen, then fall to work again furiously, as if the whole future and fortune of the pond were hanging upon his toil. After a half-hour's labour the canal was lengthened very perceptibly--fully six or eight inches--and as if by common consent the two brown excavators stopped to refresh themselves by nibbling at some succulent roots. While they were thus occupied, and apparently absorbed, from somewhere up the slope among the birch-trees came the faint sound of a snapping twig. In half a second the beavers had vanished noiselessly under water, down the canal, leaving but a swirl of muddy foam to mark their going.

CHAPTER IV

Night Watchers

WHEN the Boy came creeping down the hillside, and found the water in the canal still muddy and foaming, he realized that he had just missed a chance to see the beavers actually at work on their ditch-digging. He was disappointed. But he found ample compensation in the fact that here was one of the much-discussed and sometimes doubted canals, actually in process of construction. He knew he could outdo the beavers in their own game of wariness and watchfulness. He made up his mind he would lie out that very night, on the hillside close by--and so patiently, so unstirringly, that the beavers would never suspect the eager eyes that were upon them.

All around him, on the nearer slopes, were evidences of the purpose for which the canal was designed, as well as of the diligence with which the little people of the pond were labouring to get in their winter stores. From this diligence, so early in the season, the Boy argued an early and severe winter. He found trees of every size up to two feet in diameter cleanly felled, and stripped of their branches. With two or three exceptions--probably the work of young beavers unskilled in their art--the trees were felled unerringly in the direction of the water, so as to minimize the labour of dragging down the cuttings. Close to the new part of the canal, he found the tree whose falling he and Jabe had heard the night before. It was a tall yellow birch, fully twenty inches through at the place where it was cut, some fifteen inches from the ground. The cutting was still fresh and sappy. About half the branches had been gnawed off and trimmed, showing that the beavers, after being disturbed by the Boy's visit to the dam, had returned to work later in the night. Much of the smaller brush, from the top, had been cleared away and dragged down to the edge of the canal. As the Boy knew, from what trappers and woodsmen had told him, this brush, and a lot more like it, would all be anchored in a huge pile in mid-channel, a little above the dam, where it would serve the double purpose of breaking the force of the floods and of supplying food through the winter.

Very near the newly felled birch the Boy found another large tree about half cut through; and he vowed to himself that he would see the finish of that job that very night. He found the cutting done pretty evenly all around the tree, but somewhat lower and deeper on the side next to the water. In width the cut was less than that which a good axeman would make--because the teeth of a beaver are a more frugal cutting instrument than the woodsman's axe, making possible a straighter and less wasteful cut. At the foot of this tree he picked up chips fully eight inches in length, and was puzzled to imagine how the beavers imitated the effect of the axe in making the chips fly off.

For a couple of hours the Boy busied himself joyously, observing the work of these cunning woodsmen's teeth, noting the trails by which the remoter cuttings had been dragged down to the water, and studying the excavations on the canal. Then, fearing to make the little citizens of the pond so nervous that they might not come out to business that night, he withdrew over the slope and made his way back to camp. He would sleep out the rest of the afternoon to be fresh and keen for the night's watching.

At supper that evening, beside the camp-fire, when the woods looked magical under the still, white moon, Jabe Smith gradually got fired with the Boy's enthusiasm. The Boy's descriptions of the canal digging, of the structure of the dam, and, above all, of the battle between the otter and the beavers, filled him with a new eagerness to observe these wonderful little engineers with other eyes than those of the mere hunter and trapper. In the face of all the Boy's exact details he grew almost deferential, quite laying aside his usual backwoods pose of indifference and half derision. He made no move to go to bed, but refilled his pipe and watched his young comrade's face with shrewd, bright eyes grown suddenly boyish.

At last the Boy rose and picked up his rifle.

"I must hurry up and get myself hidden," said he, "or I'll see nothing to-night. Good night, Jabe. I'll not be back, likely, till along toward morning."

The backwoodsman's usual response was not forthcoming. For some seconds he fingered his rugged chin in silence. Then, straightening himself up, he spoke with an air of mingled embarrassment and carelessness.

"Them beaver of yourn's certainly an interestin' kind of varmint. D'ye know, blam'd if I ain't got a notion to go along with you to-night, an' watch 'em myself!"

The Boy, though secretly delighted at this evidence of something like conversion, eyed Jabe doubtfully. He was not sure of the latter's capacity for the tireless patience and long self-effacement necessary for such an adventure as this.

"Well, Jabe," he answered hesitatingly, "you know well how more than glad I'd be of your company. It would just about double my fun, having you along, if you were really interested, as I am, you know. And are you sure you could keep still long enough to see anything?"

Jabe would have resented this halting acceptance of his companionship had he not known in his heart that it was nothing more than he well deserved. But the doubt cast upon his woodcraft piqued him.

"Hain't I never set for hours in the wet ma'sh, never movin' a finger, waitin' for the geese?" he asked with injury in his voice. "Hain't I never sneaked up on a watchin' buck, or laid so still I've fooled a bear?"

The Boy chuckled softly at this outbreak, so unexpected in the taciturn and altogether superior Jabe.

"You're all right, Jabe!" said he. "I reckon you can keep still. But you must let me be captain, for to-night! This is my trick."

"Sartain," responded the woodsman with alacrity. "I'll eat mud if you say so! But I'll take along a hunk of cold bacon if you hain't got no objection."

On the trail through the ghostly, moonlit woods, Jabe followed obediently at the Boy's heels. Silently as shadows they moved, silently as the lynx or the moose or the weasel goes through the softly parting undergrowth. The Boy led far away from the brook, and over the crest of the ridge, to avoid alarming the vigilant sentries. As they approached the head of the canal, their caution redoubled, and they went very slowly, bending low and avoiding every patch of moonlight. The light breeze, so light as to be almost imperceptible, drew upward toward them from the meadow, bringing now and then a scent of the fresh-dug soil. At last the Boy lay down on his belly; and Jabe religiously imitated him. For perhaps fifty yards they crept forward inch by inch, till at length they found themselves in the heart of a young fir thicket, through whose branches they could look out upon the head of the canal and the trees where the beavers had most recently been cutting.

Among the trees and in the water, all was still, with the mystic, crystalline stillness of the autumn moonlight. In that light everything seemed fragile and unreal, as if a movement or a breath might dissolve it. After a waiting of some ten minutes Jabe had it on the tip of his tongue to whisper, derisively, "Nothin' doin'!" But he remembered the Boy's injunction, as well as his doubts, and checked himself. A moment later a faint, swirling gurgle of water caught his ear, and he was glad he had kept silence. An instant more, and the form of a beaver, spectral-gray in the moonlight, took shape all at once on the brink of the canal. For several minutes it stood there motionless, erect upon its hind quarters, questioning the stillness with eyes and ear and nose. Then, satisfied that there was no danger near, it dropped on all fours and crept up toward the tree that was partly cut through.

This pioneer of the woodcutters was followed immediately by three others, who lost no time in getting down to work. One of them went to help the leader, while the other two devoted themselves to trimming and cutting up the branches of the big birch which they had felled the night before. The Boy wondered where the rest of the pond-people were, and would have liked to consult Jabe about it; but he remembered the keenness of the beaver's ears, and held his tongue securely. It seemed to him probably that they were still down in the pond, working on the houses, the brush pile, or the dam. Presently one more was accounted for. A renewed splashing in the canal turned the attention of the watchers from the tree-cutting, and they saw that a single wise excavator was at work, carrying forward the head of the ditch.

There was no impatience or desire to fidget left in Jabe Smith now. As he watched the beavers at work in the moonlight, looking very mysterious in their stealthy, busy, tireless diligence, and conducting their toil with an ordered intelligence which seemed to him almost human, he understood for the first time the Boy's enthusiasm for this kind of bloodless hunting. He had always known how clever the beavers were, and allowed them full credit; but till now he had never actually realized it. The two beavers engaged in cutting down the tree sat erect upon their haunches, supported by their huge tails, chiseling indefatigably. Cutting two deep grooves, one about six or eight inches, perhaps, above the other, they would then wrench off the chips by main force with their teeth and forepaws, jerking their powerful necks with a kind of furious impatience. As he noted how they made the cut deeper and lower on one side than the other, that the tree might fall as they wished, he was so delighted that he came dangerously near vowing he would never trap a beaver again. He felt that it was almost like ensnaring a brother woodsman.

Equally exciting was the work on the other tree, which was being trimmed. The branches, according to their size, were cut into neat, manageable lengths, of from three to six or seven feet--the less the diameter the greater the length, each piece being calculated to be handled in the water by one beaver. These pieces were then rolled, shoved or dragged, as the case might require, down the smooth trails already made in hauling the brush, and dumped into the canal. Other beavers presently appeared, and began towing the sticks and brush down the canal to the pond. This part of the process was hidden from the eager watchers in the thicket; but the Boy guessed, from his own experience in pushing a log endwise before him while in swimming, that the beavers would handle the sticks in the same way. With the brush, however, it was different. In hauling it down the trail each beaver took a branch in his teeth, by the butt, twisted it across his shoulders, and let it drag behind him. It was obvious that in the water, too, this would be the most convenient way to handle such material. The beavers were not the kind of people to waste their strength in misdirected effort.

While all this cutting and hauling was going on, the big beaver down at the head of the canal was attending strictly to his task, running his lines straight, digging the turf and clay, shoving his loads up the slope and out upon the edge of the ditch. The process was all in clear, easy view of the watchers, their place of hiding being not more than eight or ten paces distant.

They had grown altogether absorbed in watching the little canal-builder, when a cracking sound made them turn their eyes. The tree was toppling slowly. Every beaver now made a mad rush for the canal, not caring how much noise he made--and plunged into the water. Slowly, reluctantly, majestically, the tall birch swung forward straight down the slope, its top describing a great arc against the sky and gathering the air in its branches with a low but terrifying roar. The final crash was unexpectedly gentle,--or rather, would have seemed so to one unfamiliar with tree-felling. Some branches snapped, some sticks flew up and dropped, there was a shuddering confusion in the crystal air for a few seconds, then the stillness fell once more.

But now there was not a beaver to be seen. Jabe wondered if they had been scared by the results of their own work; or if one of their sentinels had come and peered into the thicket from the rear. As minute after minute dragged by, and nothing happened, he began to realize that his muscles were aching savagely from their long restraint. He was on the point of moving, of whispering to ask the Boy what it meant, when the latter, divining his unrest, stealthily laid a restraining hand upon his arm. He guessed that the beavers were on the alert, hiding, and watching to see if any of their enemies should be attracted by the noise.

Not five seconds later, however, he forgot his aches. Appearing with uncanny and inexplicable suddenness, there was the big pioneer again, sitting up by the edge of the canal. As before, he sat absolutely motionless for a minute or two, sniffing and listening. Then, satisfied once more that all was well, he moved lazily up the slope to examine the tree; and in half a minute all were at work again, except that there was no more tree-felling. The great business of the hour was cutting brush.

For some time longer the watchers lay motionless, noting every detail of the work, till at last the Boy began to think it was time to release Jabe from his long and severe restraint and break up the beaver "chopping-bee." Before he had quite made up his mind, however, his eyes chanced to wander a little way up the slope, and to rest, without any conscious purpose, on a short gray bit of log. Presently he began to wonder what a piece of log so short and thick--not much more than three feet long--would be doing there. No beavers would waste time cutting up a twelve-inch log into lengths like that. And there had been no lumberman in the neighbourhood. Then, in a flash, his eyes cleared themselves of their illusion. The log had moved, ever so slightly. It was no longer a log, but a big gray lynx, creeping slowly, inexorably, down upon the unsuspecting people of the pond.

For perhaps ten seconds the Boy stared in uncertainty. Then he saw the lynx gather his muscles for the final, fatal rush. Without a whisper or a warning to the astonished Jabe, he whipped up his rifle, and fired.

The sharp report seemed to shatter the whole scene. Its echoes were mixed with the scattering of the horrified beavers as they rushed for the water--with the short screech of the lynx, as it bounced into the air and fell back on its side, dead--with an exclamation of astonishment from Jabe--and with a crashing of branches just behind the thicket. The Boy looked around, triumphant--to see that Jabe's exclamation was not at all the result of his clever shot. The woodsman was on his hands and knees, his back turned, and staring at the form of a big black bear as it lumbered off in a panic through the bushes. Like the unfortunate lynx, the bear had been stalking the beavers on his own account, and had almost stepped upon the silent watchers in the thicket.

CHAPTER V

Dam Repairing and Dam Building

AS the Boy trudged triumphantly back toward camp, over the crest of the moon-bright ridge, he carried the limp, furry body of the lynx slung by its hind legs over his shoulder. He felt that his prestige had gone up incalculably in the woodsman's eyes. The woodsman was silent, however, as silent as the wilderness, till they descended the other slope and came in sight of the little solitary camp. Then he said: "That was a mighty slick shot of yourn, d'ye know it? Ye're quicker'n chain lightnin', an' dead on!"

"Just luck, Jabe!" replied the Boy carelessly, trying to seem properly modest.

This different suggestion Jabe did not take the trouble to controvert. He knew the Boy did not mean it.

"But I thought as how ye wouldn't kill anything?" he went on, teasingly.

"Had to!" retorted the Boy. "That was self-defence! Those beavers are my beavers. An' I've always wanted a real good excuse for getting a good lynx skin, anyway!"

"I don't blame ye a mite fer standin' by them beaver!" continued Jabe. "They're jest all right! It was better'n any circus; an' I don't know when I've enjoyed myself more."

"Then the least you can do, Jabe, is promise not to trap any more beavers!" said the Boy quickly.

"Wa'al," answered Jabe, as they entered camp and began spreading their blankets, "leastwise I'll do my best to see that no harm comes to them beaver, nor to the pond."

Next morning, as the woodsman was starting out for the day's cruise, the Boy said to him:

"If you're game for another night's watching, Jabe, I'll show you something altogether different up at the pond to-night."

"Try me!" responded the woodsman.

"You'll have to be back earlier than usual, then," said the Boy. "We'll have to get hidden earlier, and in a new place."

"I'll come back along a couple of hours afore sundown, then," answered Jabe, swinging off on his long, mooselike stride. It was contrary to his backwoods etiquette to ask what was in store for him; but his curiosity was excited, and kept him company through the solitude all day.

When Jabe was gone, the Boy went straight up-stream to the dam, taking no special care to hide his coming. His plan was one in regard to which he felt some guilty qualms. But he consoled himself with the thought that whatever harm he might be doing to the little citizens of the pond would be more than compensated by the protection he was giving them. He was going to make a break in the dam, for the sake of seeing just how the beavers would mend it.

On reaching the dam, however, it occurred to him that if he made the break now the beavers might regard the matter as too urgent to be left till nightfall. They might steal a march on him by mending the damage little by little, surreptitiously, through the day. He had no way of knowing just how they would take so serious a danger as a break in their dam. He decided, therefore, to postpone his purpose till the afternoon, so that the beavers would not come to the rescue too early. In the meantime, he would explore the stream above the pond, and see if there were other communities to study.

Skirting the hither side of the pond to near its head, he crossed the little meadow and the canal, and reached the brook again about fifty yards beyond. Here he found it flowing swift and narrow, over a rocky bottom, between high banks; and this was its character for nearly half a mile, as he judged. Then, emerging once more upon lower ground, he came upon a small dam. This structure was not much over eighteen inches in height, and the pond above it, small and shallow, showed no signs of being occupied. There was no beaver house to be seen, either in the water or on shore; and the water did not seem to be anywhere more than a foot and a half in depth. As he puzzled over this--for he did not think the beavers were likely to build a dam for nothing--he observed a second and much larger dam far away across the head of the pond.

Hastening to investigate this upper dam, he found it fully three feet high, and very massive. Above it was a narrow but deep pond, between comparatively steep shores; and along these shores he counted three low-roofed houses. Out in the middle of the pond there was not one dwelling; and he came presently to the conclusion that here, between the narrow banks, the current would be heavy in time of freshet. The lower dam, pretty obviously, was intended to reinforce the upper, by backing a foot and a half of water against it and taking off just that much of the pressure. He decided that the reason for locating the three houses along the shore was that the steep bank afforded special facilities for shore burrows.

The explorer's fever being now hot upon him, the Boy could not stay to examine this pond minutely. He pressed on up-stream with breathless eagerness, thrilling with expectation of what the next turn might reveal. As a matter of fact, the next turn revealed nothing--nor the next, nor yet the next. But as the stream was full of turns in this portion of its course, that was not greatly discouraging.

About a quarter of a mile, however, above the head of the narrow pond, the ardent explorer came upon a level of sparse alder swamp. Here he found the stream just beginning to spread over its low banks. The cause of this spreading was a partial obstruction in mid-channel--what looked, at first glance, like an accidental accumulation of brush and stones and mud. A second look, however, and his heart jumped with excitement and delight. Here was the beginning of a new pond, here were the foundations of a new dam. He would be able to see what few indeed of the students of the wilderness had had the opportunity to watch--the actual process by which these wilderness engineers achieved their great work.

All about the place the straightest and brushiest alders had been cut down, those usually selected being at least ten or twelve feet in height. Many of them were still lying where they fell; but a number had been dragged to the stream and anchored securely, with stones and turfy clay, across the channel. The Boy noted, with keenest admiration, that these were all laid with the greatest regularity parallel with the flow of the current, butts up stream, brushy tops below. In this way, the current took least hold upon them, and was obstructed gradually and as it were insidiously, without being challenged to any violent test of strength. Already it was lingering in some confusion, backing up, and dividing its force, and stealing away at each side among the bushes. The Boy had heard that the beavers were accustomed to begin their dams by felling a tree across the channel and piling their materials upon that as a foundation. But the systematic and thorough piece of work before him was obviously superior in permanence to any such slovenly makeshift; and moreover, further to discredit such a theory, here was a tall black ash close to the stream and fairly leaning over it, as if begging to be put to some such use.

At this spot the Boy stayed his explorations for the day. Choosing a bit of dry thicket close by, to be a hiding-place for Jabe and himself that night, a bunch of spruce and fir where he knew the beavers would not come for supplies, he hurried back to the camp for a bite of dinner, giving wide berth to all the ponds on the way. Building a tiny camp-fire he fried himself a couple of slices of bacon and brewed a tin of tea for his solitary meal, then lay down in the lean-to, with the sun streaming in upon him, for an hour's nap.

The night having been a tiring one for his youthful nerves and muscles, he slept heavily, and awoke with a start to find the sun a good two hours nearer the horizon. Sleep was still heavy upon him, so he went down to the edge of the brook and plunged his face into the chilly current. Then, picking up an axe instead of his rifle, he returned up-stream to the dam.

As he drew near, he caught sight of a beaver swimming down the pond, towing a big branch over its shoulder; and his conscience smote him at the thought of the trouble and anxiety he was going to inflict upon the diligent little inhabitants. His mind was made up, however. He wanted knowledge, and the beavers would have to furnish it, at whatever cost. A few minutes of vigorous work with the axe, a few minutes of relentless tugging and jerking upon the upper framework of the dam, and he had made a break through which the water rushed foaming in a muddy torrent. Soon, as he knew, the falling of the pond's level would alarm the house-dwellers, and bring them out to see what had happened. Then, as soon as darkness came, there would be a gathering of both households to repair the break.

Hiding in the bushes near by, he saw the water slowly go down, but for half an hour the beavers gave no sign. Then, close beside the break, a big fellow crawled out upon the slope of the dam and made a careful survey of the damage. He disappeared; and presently another came, took a briefer look, and vanished. A few minutes later, far up the pond, several bushy branches came to the surface, as if they had been anchored on the bottom and released. They came, apparently floating, down toward the dam. As they reached the break, the heads of several beavers showed themselves above water, and the branches were guided across the opening, where they were secured in some way which the watcher could not see. They did not so very greatly diminish the waste, but they checked the destructive violence of it. It was evidently a temporary makeshift, this; for in the next hour nothing more was done. Then the Boy got tired, and went back to camp to wait for Jabe and nightfall.

That evening the backwoodsman, forgetting the fatigue of his day's cruising in the interest of the Boy's story, was no less eager than his companion; and the two, hurrying through an early supper, were off for the pond in the first purple of twilight. When they reached the Boy's hiding-place by the dam the first star was just showing itself in the pallid greenish sky, and the surface of the pond, with its vague, black reflections, was like a shadowed mirror of steel. There was not a sound on the air except the swishing rush of the divided water over the break in the dam.

The Boy had timed his coming none too early; for the pond had dropped nearly a foot, and the beavers were impatient to stop the break. No sooner had night fairly settled down than suddenly the water began to swirl into circles all about the lower end of the pond, and a dozen heads popped up. Then more brush appeared, above the island-house, and was hurriedly towed down to the dam. The brush which had been thrust across the break was now removed and relaid longitudinally, branchy ends down stream. Here it was held in place by some of the beavers while others brought masses of clayey turf from the nearest shore to secure it. Meanwhile more branches were being laid in place, always parallel with the current; and in a little while the rushing noise of the overflow began to diminish very noticeably. Then a number of short, heavy billets were mixed with shorter lengths of brush; and all at once the sound of rushing ceased altogether. There was not even the usual musical trickling and tinkling, for the level of the pond was too low for the water to find its customary stealthy exits. At this stage the engineers began using smaller sticks, with more clay, and a great many small stones, making a very solid-looking piece of work. At last the old level of the dam crest was reached, and there was no longer any evidence of what had happened except the lowness of the water. Then, all at once, the toilers disappeared, except for one big beaver, who kept nosing over every square inch of the work for perhaps two minutes, to assure himself of its perfection. When he, at last, had slipped back into the water, both Jabe and the Boy got up, as if moved by one thought, and stretched their cramped legs.

"I swan!" exclaimed the woodsman with fervour. "If that ain't the slickest bit o' work I ever seen! Let's go over and kind of inspect the job fer 'em!"

Inspection revealed that the spot which had just been mended was the solidest portion of the whole structure. Wherever else the water might be allowed to escape, it was plain the beavers intended it should have no more outlet here.

From the mended dam the Boy now led Jabe away up-stream in haste, in the hope of catching some beavers at work on the new dam in the alders. Having skirted the long pond at a distance, to avoid giving alarm, the travellers went with the utmost caution till they reached the swampy level. Then, indifferent to the oozy, chilly mud, they crept forward like minks stealing on their prey; and at last, gaining the fir thicket without mishap, they lay prone on the dry needles to rest.

As they lay, a sound of busy splashing came to their ears, which promptly made them forget their fatigue. Shifting themselves very slowly and with utter silence, they found that the place of ambush had been most skilfully chosen. In perfect hiding themselves, they commanded a clear and near view of the new dam and all its approaches.

There were two beavers visible, paddling busily on the foundations of the dam, while the overflowing water streamed about them, covering their feet. At this stage, most of the water flowed through the still uncompacted structure, leaving work on the top unimpeded. The two beavers were dragging into place a long birch sapling, perhaps eleven feet in length, with a thick, bushy top. When laid to the satisfaction of the architects,--the butt, of course, pointing straight up-stream,--the trunk was jammed firmly down between those already placed. Then the more erect and unmanageable of the branches were gnawed off and in some way--which the observers with all their watchfulness could not make out--wattled down among the other branches so as to make a woven and coherent mass. The earth and sod and small stones which were afterwards brought and laid upon the structure did not seem necessary to hold it in place, but rather for the stoppage of the interstices.

While this was going on at the dam, a rustling of branches and splashing of water turned the watchers' attention up-stream. Another beaver came in sight, and then another, each partly floating and partly dragging a straight sapling like the first. It seemed that the dam-builders were not content to depend altogether on the crooked, scraggly alder-growth all about them, but demanded in their foundations a certain proportion of the straighter timbers and denser branches of the birch. It was quite evident that they knew just what they were doing, and how best to do it.

While the building was going on, yet another pair of beavers appeared, and the work was pressed with a feverish energy that produced amazing results. The Boy remembered a story told him by an old Indian, but not confirmed by any natural history which he had come across, to the effect that when a pair of young beavers set out to establish a new pond, some of the old ones go along to lend a hand in the building of the dam. It was plain that these workers were all in a tremendous hurry; and the Boy could see no reason for haste unless it was that the majority of the workers had to get back to their own affairs. With the water once fairly brought under control, and the pond deep enough to afford a refuge from enemies, the young pair could be trusted to complete it by themselves, get their house ready, and gather their supplies in for the winter. The Boy concluded to his own satisfaction that what he was now watching was the analogue, in beaver life, to one of those "house-raising" bees which sometimes took place in the Settlement, when the neighbours would come together to help a man get up the frame of a new house. Only, as it seemed to him, the beavers were a more serious and more sober folk than the men.

When this wilderness engineering had progressed for an hour under the watchers' eyes, Jabe began to grow very tired. The strain of physical immobility told upon him, and he lost interest. He began to feel that he knew all about dam-building; and as there was nothing more to learn he wanted to go back to camp. He glanced anxiously at the young face beside him--but there he could see no sign of weariness. The Boy was aglow with enthusiasm. He had forgotten everything but the wonderful little furry architects, their diligence, their skill, their co 鰭 eration, and the new pond there growing swiftly before his eyes. Already it was more than twice as wide as when they had arrived on the scene; the dam was a good eight inches higher; and the clamour of the flowing stream was stopped. No, Jabe could see no sympathy for himself in that eager face. He was ashamed to beg off. And moreover, he was loyal to his promise of obedience. The Boy, here, was Captain.

Suppressing a sigh, Jabe stealthily and very gradually shifted to an easier position, so stealthily that the Boy beside him did not know he had moved. Then, fixing his eyes once more upon the beavers, he tried to renew his interest in them. As he stared, he began to succeed amazingly. And no wonder! The beavers all at once began to do such amazing things. There were many more of them than he had thought; and he was sure he heard them giving orders in something that sounded to him like the Micmac tongue. He could not believe his ears. Then he saw that they were using larger stones, instead of mud and turf, in their operations--and floating them down the pond as if they were corks. He had never heard of such a thing before, in all his wilderness experience. He was just about to compliment the Boy on this unparalleled display of engineering skill, when one particularly large beaver, who was hoisting a stone as big as himself up the face of the dam, let his burden slip a little. Then began a terrible struggle between the beaver and the stone. In his agonizing effort--which his companions all stopped work to watch--the unhappy beaver made a loud, gurgling, gasping noise; then, without a hint of warning, dropped the stone with a splash, turned like lightning, and grabbed Jabe violently by the arm.

The astonishing scene changed in a twinkling; and Jabe realized that the Boy was shaking him.

"A nice one to watch beavers, you are!" cried the Boy, angry and disappointed.

"Why--where've they all gone to?" demanded Jabe, rubbing his eyes. "They're the most interestin' critters I ever hearn tell of!"

"Interesting!" retorted the Boy, scornfully. "So interesting you went to sleep! And you snored so they thought it was an earthquake. Not another beaver'll show a hair round here to-night. We'd better go home!"

Jabe grinned sheepishly, but answered never a word; and silently, in Indian file, the Boy leading, the two took the trail back to camp.

CHAPTER VI

The Peril of the Traps

AT breakfast next morning the Boy had quite recovered his good humour, and was making merry at Jabe's expense. The latter, who was, of course, defenceless and abashed, was anxious to give him something new to think of.

"Say," he exclaimed suddenly, after the Boy had prodded him with a searching jibe. "If ye'll let up on that snore, now, I'll take a day off from my cruisin', and show ye somethin' myself."

"Good!" said the Boy. "It's a bargain. What will you show me?"

"I'll take ye over to one of my ponds, in next valley, an' show ye all the different ways of trappin' beaver."

The Boy's face fell.

"But what do I care about trapping beaver?" he cried. "You know I wouldn't trap anything. If I had to kill anything, I'd shoot it, and put it out of misery as quick as I could!"

"I know all that," responded Jabe. "But trappin' is somethin' ye want to understand, all the same. Ye can't be an all-round woodsman 'less ye understand trappin'. An' moreover, there's some things ye learn about wild critters in tryin' to git the better of 'em that ye can't learn no other way."

"I guess you're right, Jabe!" answered the Boy, slowly. Knowledge he would have, whether he liked the means of getting it or not. But the woodsman's next words relieved him.

"I'll just show ye how, that's all!" said Jabe. "It's a leetle too airly in the season yit fur actual trappin'. An' moreover, it's agin the law. Agin the law, an' agin common sense, too, fer the fur ain't no good, so to speak, fer a month yit. When the law an' common sense stand together, then I'm fer the law. Come on!"

Picking up his axe, he struck straight back into the woods, in a direction at right angles to the brook. To uninitiated eyes there was no trail; but to Jabe, and to the Boy no less, the path was like a trodden highway. The pace set by the backwoodsman, with his long, slouching, loose-jointed, flat-footed stride, was a stiff one, but the Boy, who was lean and hard, and used his feet straight-toed like an Indian, had no fault to find with it. Neither spoke a word, as they swung along single file through the high-arched and ancient forest, whose shadows, so sombre all through summer, were now shot here and there with sharp flashes of scarlet or pale gleams of aerial gold. Once, rounding a great rock of white granite stained with faint pinkish and yellowish reflections from the bright leaves glowing over it, they came face to face with a tall bull moose, black and formidable-looking as some antediluvian monster. The monster, however, had no desire to hold the way against them. He eyed them doubtfully for a second, and then went crashing off through the brush in frank, undignified alarm.

For a good three miles the travellers swung onward, up a slow long slope, and down a longer, slower one into the next valley. The Boy noted that the region was one of numberless small brooks flowing through a comparatively level land, with old, long-deserted beaver-meadows interspersed among wooded knolls. Yet for a time there were no signs of the actual living beavers. He asked the reason, and Jabe said:

"It's been all trapped over an' over, years back, when beaver pelts was high,--an' by Injuns, likely, who just cleaned out everythin',--an' broke down the dams,--an' dug out the houses. But the little critters is comin' back. Furder up the valley there's some good ponds now!"

"And now they'll be cleaned out again!" exclaimed the Boy, with a rush of indignant pity.

"Not on yer life!" answered Jabe. "We don't do things that way now. We don't play low-down tricks on 'em an' clean out a whole family, but jest take so many out of each beaver house, an' then leave 'em alone two er three years to kinder recooperate!"

As Jabe finished they came in sight of a long, rather low dam, with a pond spread out beyond it that was almost worthy to be called a lake. It was of comparatively recent creation, as the Boy's observant eye decided at once from the dead trees still rising here and there from the water.

"Gee!" he exclaimed, under his breath. "That's a great pond, Jabe!"

"There's no less'n four beaver houses in that pond!" said the woodsman, with an air of proud possession. "That makes, accordin' to my reckonin', anywheres from thirty to thirty-six beaver. Bye and bye, when the time comes, I'll kinder thin 'em out a bit, that's all!"

From the crest of the dam all four houses--one far out and three close to shore--were visible to the Boy's initiated eye; though strangers might have taken them to be mere casual accumulations of sticks deposited by some whimsical freshet. It troubled him to think how many of the architects of these cunningly devised dwellings would soon have to yield up their harmless and interesting lives; but he felt no mission to attempt a reform of humanity's taste for furs, so he did not allow himself to become sentimental on the subject. Beavers, like men, must take fate as it comes; and he turned an attentive ear to Jabe's lesson.

"Ye know, of course," said the woodsman, "the steel trap we use. We ain't got no use fer the tricks of the Injuns, though I'm goin' to tell ye all them, in good time. An' we ain't much on new-fangled notions, neether. But the old, smooth-jawed steel-trap, what kin hold when it gits a grip, an' not tear the fur, is good enough for us."

"Yes, I know all your traps, of all the sizes you use, from muskrat up to bear!" interrupted the Boy. "What size do you use for the beaver?"

"Number four," answered Jabe. "Jaw's got a spread of six and one-half inches or thereabouts. But it's all in the where an' the how ye set yer trap!"

"And that's what I want to know about!" said the Boy. "But why don't you shoot the poor little beggars? That's quicker for both, and just as easy for you, ain't it?"

"T'ain't no use shootin' a beaver, leastways not in the water! He just sinks like a stone. No, ye've got to trap him, to git him. Now, supposin' you was goin' to trap, where would ye set the traps?"

"I'd anchor them just in the entrances to their houses," answered the Boy promptly. "Or along their canals, when they've got canals. Or round their brush piles an' storage heaps. And when I found a tree they'd just partly cut down, I'd set a couple of traps, covered up in leaves, each side of the trunk, where they'd have to step on the pan when they stood up to gnaw."

"Good for you!" said Jabe, with cordial approbation. "Ye'd make a first-class trapper, 'cause ye've got the right notion. Every one of them things is done, one time or another, by the old trapper. But here's one or two wrinkles more killin' yet. An' moreover, if ye trap a beaver on land ye're like to lose him one way or another. He's got so much purchase, on land, with things to git hold on to; he's jest as like as not to twist his leg clean off, an' git away. If it's one of his fore legs, which is small an' slight, ye know, he's most sure to twist it off. An' sometimes he'll do the trick even with a hind leg. I've caught lots of beaver as had lost a fore leg, an' didn't seem none the worse. The fur'd growed over it, an' they was slick an' hearty. An' I've caught them as had lost a hind leg, an' they was in good condition. A beaver'll stand a lot, I tell you. But then, supposin' you git yer beaver, caught so fast he ain't no chance whatever to git clear. Then, like as not, some lynx, or wildcat, or fisher, or fox, or even maybe a bear, 'll come along an' help himself to Mr. Beaver without so much as a by yer leave. No, ye want to git him in the water; an' as he's just as anxious to git thar as you are to git him thar, that suits all parties to a T."

[Illustration: "'OR EVEN MAYBE A BEAR.'"]

"Good!" said the Boy,--not that it really seemed to him good, but to show that he was attending.

"But," continued Jabe, "what would ye say would most upset the beaver and make 'em careless?"

The Boy thought for a moment.

"Breaking their dam!" he answered tentatively.

"Egzactly!" answered the woodsman. "Well, now, to ketch beaver sure, make two or three breaks in their dam, an' set the traps jest a leetle ways above the break, on the upper slope, where they're sure to step into 'em when hustlin' round to mend the damage. That gits 'em, every time. Ye chain each trap to a stake, driven into three or four foot of water; an' ye drive another stake about a foot an' a half away from the first. When the beaver finds himself caught, he dives straight for deep water,--his way of gittin' clear of most of his troubles. But this time he finds it don't work. The trap keeps a holt, bitin' hard. An' in his struggle he gits the chain all tangled up 'round the two stakes, an' drowns himself. There you have him safe, where no lynx nor fox kin git at him."

"Then, when one of them dies so dreadfully, right there before their eyes," said the Boy, "I suppose the others skin out and let the broken dam go! They must be scared to death themselves!"

"Not on yer life, they don't!" responded Jabe. "The dam's the thing they care about. They jest keep on hustlin' round; an' they mend up that dam if it takes half the beaver in the pond to do it. Oh, they're grit, all right, when it comes to standin' by the dam."

"Hardly seems fair to take them that way, does it?" mused the Boy sympathetically.

"It's a good way," asserted Jabe positively, "quick an' sure! Then, in winter there's another good an' sure way,--where ye don't want to clean out the whole house, which is killin' the goose what lays the golden egg, like the Injuns does! Ye cut a hole in the ice, near the bank. Then ye git a good, big, green sapling of birch or willow, run the little end 'way out into the pond under the ice, an' ram the big end, sharpened, deep into the mud of the bank, so the beaver can't pull it out. Right under this end you set yer trap. Swimmin' round under the ice, beaver comes across this fresh-cut sapling an' thinks as how he's got a good thing. He set right to work to gnaw it off, close to the bank, to take it back to the house an' please the family. First thing, he steps right into the trap. An' that's the end of him. But other beaver'll come along an' take the sapling, all the same!"

"You spoke of the ways the Indians had, of cleaning out the whole family," suggested the Boy, when Jabe had come to a long pause, either because he was tired of talking or because he had no more to say.

"Yes, the Injuns' methods was complete. They seemed to have the idee there'd always be beaver a-plenty, no matter how many they killed. One way they had was to mark down the bank holes, the burrows, an' then break open the houses. This, ye must understand, 's in the winter, when there's ice all over the pond. When they're drove from their houses, in the winter, they take straight to their burrows in the bank, where they kin be sure of gittin' their heads above water to breathe. Then, the Injuns jest drive stakes down in front of the holes,--an' there they have 'em, every one. They digs down into the burrows, an' knocks Mr. Beaver an' all the family on the head."

"Simple and expeditious!" remarked the Boy, with sarcastic approval.

"But the nestest job the Injuns makes," continued Jabe, "is by gittin' at the brush pile. Ye know, the beaver keeps his winter supply of grub in a pile,--a pile of green poles an' saplings an' branches,--a leetle ways off from the house. The Injun finds this pile, under the ice. Then, cuttin' holes through the ice, he drives down a stake fence all 'round it, so close nary a beaver kin git through. Then he pulls up a stake, on the side next the beaver house, an' sticks down a bit of a sliver in its place. Now ye kin guess what happens. In the house, over beyant, the beavers gits hungry. One on 'em goes to git a stick from the pile an' bring it inter the house. He finds the pile all fenced off. But a stick he must have. Where the sliver is, that's the only place he kin git through. Injun, waitin' on the ice, sees the sliver move, an' knows Mr. Beaver's gone in. He claps the stake down agin, in place of the sliver. An' then, of course, there's nawthin' left fer Mr. Beaver to do but drown. He drowns jest at the place where he come in an' couldn't git out agin. That seems to knock him out, like, an' he jest gives up right there. Injun fishes him out, dead, puts the sliver back, an' waits for another beaver. He don't have to wait long-- an' nine times outer ten he gits 'em all. Ye see, they must git to the brush pile!"

[Illustration: "HE DROWNS JEST AT THE PLACE WHERE HE COME IN."]

"I'm glad you don't trap them that way, Jabe!" said the Boy. "But tell me, why did you bring me away out here to this pond, to tell me all this, when you could have done it just as well at my pond?"

"I jest wanted the excuse," answered Jabe, "fer takin' a day off from cruisin'. Now, come on, an' I'll show ye some more likely ponds."

CHAPTER VII

Winter Under Water

FOR three days more the Boy and Jabe remained in the beaver country; and every hour of the time, except when he had to sleep, the Boy found full of interest. In the daytime he compared the ponds and the dams minutely, making measurements and diagrams. At night he lay in hiding, beside a different pond each night, and gained a rich store of knowledge of the manners and customs of the little wilderness engineers. On one pond--his own, be it said--he made a rude raft of logs, and by its help visited and inspected the houses on the island. The measurements he obtained here made his note-book pretty complete, as far as beaver life in summer and fall was concerned.

Then Jabe finished his cruising, having covered his territory. The packs were made up and slung; the two campers set out on their three days' tramp back to the settlements; and the solemn autumn quiet descended once more upon the placid beaver ponds, the shallow-running brooks, and the low-domed Houses in the Water.

As the weather grew colder; and the earlier frosts began to sheathe the surface of the pond with clear, black ice, not melting out till noon; and the bitten leaves, turning from red and gold to brown, fell with ghostly whisperings through the gray branches, the little beaver colony in Boy's Pond grew feverishly active. Some subtle prescience warned them that winter would close in early, and that they must make haste to finish their storing of supplies. The lengthening of their new canal completed, their foraging grew easier. Trees fell every night, and the brush pile reached a size that guaranteed them immunity from hunger till spring. By the time the dam had been strengthened to withstand the late floods, there had been some sharp snow-flurries, and the pond was half frozen over. Then, in haste, the beavers brought up a quantity of mud and grass roots, and plastered the domes of their houses thickly till they no longer looked like heaps of sticks, but rather resembled huge ant-hills. No sooner was this task done than, as if the beavers had been notified of its coming, the real cold came. In one night the pond froze to a depth of several inches; and over the roof of the House in the Water was a casing of armour hard as stone.

The frost continued for several days, till the stone-like roof was a good foot in thickness, as was the ice over the surface of the pond. Then a thick, feather-soft, windless snow-fall, lasting twenty-four hours, served as a blanket against the further piercing of the frost; and the beavers, warm-housed, well-provisioned, and barricaded against all their enemies but man, settled themselves down to their long seclusion from the white, glittering, bitter, outside world.

When the winter had tightened its grip, this outside world was full of perils. Hungry lynxes, foxes, and fishers ("black cat," the woodsman called them) hunted through the silent and pallid aisles of the forest. They all would have loved a meal of warm, fat beaver-meat; and they all knew what these low, snow-covered mounds meant. In the roof of each house the cunning builders had left several tiny, crooked openings for ventilation, and the warm air steaming up through these made little chimney holes in the snow above. To these, now and then, when stung by the hunger-pangs, a lynx or fox would come, and sniff with greedy longing at the appetizing aroma. Growing desperate, the prowler would dig down, through perhaps three feet of snow, till he reached the stony roof of the house. On this he would tear and scratch furiously, but in vain. Nothing less than a pick-axe would break through that stony defence; and the beavers, perhaps dimly aware of the futile assault upon their walls, would go on calmly nibbling birch-sticks in their safe, warm dark.

Inside the house everything was clean and dry. All refuse from the clean repasts of the family was scrupulously removed, and even the entrances, far out in the pond, were kept free from litter. When food was needed, a beaver would slip down into the dark water of the tunnel, out into the glimmering light of the pond, and straight to the brush pile. Selecting a suitable stick, he would tow it back to the house, up the main entrance, and into the dry, dark chamber. When all the tender bark was eaten off, the bare stick would be carried away and deposited on the dam. It was an easy life; and the beavers grew fat while all the rest of the wild kindreds, save the porcupine and the bear, were growing lean with famine. There was absolutely nothing to do but eat, sleep and take such exercise as they would by swimming hither and thither at terrific speed beneath the silver armour of the ice.

One night, however, there came to the pond an enemy of whose powers they had never had experience. Wandering down from northwestward, under the impulse of one of those migratory whims which sometimes give the lie to statistics and tradition, came a sinister, dark, slow-moving beast whose savage and crafty eyes took on a sudden flame when they detected the white mound which hid the shore beaver-house. The wolverene did not need that faint, almost invisible wisp of vapour from the air-holes to tell him there were beavers below. He knew something about beavers. His powerful forearms and mighty claws got him to the bottom of the snow in a few seconds. Other hungry marauders had done the same thing before, to find themselves as far off as ever from their aim. But the wolverene was not to be balked so easily. His cunning nose found the minute openings of the air-holes; and by digging his claws into these little apertures he was able to put forth his great strength and tear up some tiny fragments of frozen mud.

If he had had the patience to keep on at his strenuous task unremittingly for, perhaps, twenty-four hours or more, it is conceivable that this fierce digger might have succeeded in making his way into the chamber. There was no such implacable purpose, however, in his attack. In a very little while he would have desisted from what he knew to be a vain undertaking. Even had he succeeded, the beavers would have fled before he could reach them, and taken refuge in their burrows under the bank. But while he was still engrossed, perhaps only amusing himself with the thought of giving the dwellers in the house a bad quarter of an hour, it chanced that a huge lynx came stealing along through the shadows of the trees, which lay blue and spectral in the white moonlight. He saw the hind quarters of some unknown animal which was busy working out a problem which he himself had striven in vain to solve. The strange animal was plainly smaller than himself. Moreover, he was in a position to be taken at a disadvantage. Both these points weighed with the lynx; and he was enraged at this attempted poaching upon what he chose to regard as his preserves. Creeping stealthily, stealthily forward, eyes aflame and belly to the snow, he sprang with a huge bound that landed him, claws open, squarely on the wolverene's hind quarters.

Instantly there arose a hideous screeching, growling, spitting and snarling, which pierced even to the ears of the beavers and sent them scurrying wildly to their burrows in the bank. Under ordinary circumstances the wolverene, with his dauntless courage and tremendous strength, would have given a good account of himself with any lynx alive. But this time, caught with head down and very busy, he stood small chance with his powerful and lightning-swift assailant. In a very few minutes the lynx's eviscerating claws had fairly torn him to shreds; and thus came to a sudden close the invasion of the wolverene.

But meanwhile, from far over the hills, moving up from the lowlands by the sea, approached a peril which the beavers did not dream of and could find no ingenuity to evade. Two half-breed trappers, semi-outlaws from the Northern Peninsula, in search of fresh hunting-grounds, had come upon this rich region of ponds and dams.

CHAPTER VIII

The Saving of Boy's Pond

WHEN, early in the winter, the lumbermen moved into these woods which Jabe had cruised over, establishing their camp about two miles down-stream from the spot where the Boy and the woodsman had had their lean-to, Jabe came with them as boss of a gang. He had for the time grown out of the mood for trapping. Furs were low, and there was a "sight" more money for him in lumbering that winter. Popular with the rest of the lumbermen--who most of them knew of the Boy and his "queer" notions--Jabe had no difficulty in pledging them to respect the sanctity of Boy's Pond and its inhabitants. In fact, in the evenings around the red-hot stove, Jabe told such interesting stories of what he and the Boy had seen together a few months before, that the reckless, big-hearted, boisterously profane but sentimental woodsmen were more than half inclined to declare the whole series of ponds under the special protection of the camp. As for Boy's Pond, that should be safe at any cost.

Not long after Christmas the Boy, taking advantage of the fact that some fresh supplies were being sent out from the Settlement by team, came to visit the camp. The head of the big lumber company which owned these woods was a friend of the Boy's father, and the Boy himself was welcome in any of the camps. His special purpose in coming now was to see how his beavers got on in winter, and to assure himself that Jabe had been able to protect them.

The morning after his arrival in camp he set out to visit the pond. He went on snowshoes, of course, and carried his little Winchester as he always did in the woods, holding tenaciously that the true lover of peace should be ever prepared for war. The lumbermen had gone off to work with the first of dawn; and far away to his right he heard the axes ringing, faintly but crisply, on the biting morning air. For half a mile he followed a solitary snowshoe trail, which he knew to be Jabe's by the peculiar broad toe and long, trailing heel which Jabe affected in snowshoes; and he wondered what his friend was doing in this direction, so far from the rest of the choppers. Then Jabe's track swerved off to the left, crossing the brook; and the Boy tramped on over the unbroken snow.

The sound of the distant choppers soon died away, and he was alone in the unearthly silence. The sun, not yet risen quite clear of the hilltops, sent spectral, level, far-reaching gleams of thin pink-and-saffron light down the alleys of the sheeted trees. The low crunching of his snowshoes on the crisp snow sounded almost blatant in the Boy's tensely listening ears. In spite of himself he began to tread stealthily, as if the sound of his steps might bring some ghostly enemy upon him from out of the whiteness.

Suddenly the sound of an axe came faintly to his ears from straight ahead, where he knew no choppers were at work. He stopped short. That axe was not striking wood. It was striking ice. It was chopping the ice of Boy's Pond! What could it mean? There were no fish in that pond to chop the ice for!

As he realized that some one was preparing to trap his beavers his face flushed with anger, and he started forward at a run. That it was no one from the camp he knew very well. It must be some strange trapper who did not know that this pond was under protection. He thought this out as he ran on; and his anger calmed down. Trappers were a decent, understanding folk; and a word of explanation would make things all right. There were plenty of other beaver ponds in that neighbourhood.

Pressing through the white-draped ranks of the young fir-trees, he came out suddenly upon the edge of the pond, and halted an instant in irresolution. Two dark-visaged men--his quick eye knew them for half-breeds--were busy on the snow about twenty paces above the low mound which marked the main beaver house. They had a number of stakes with them; and they were cutting a series of holes in a circle. From what Jabe had told him of the Indian methods, he saw at once that these were not regular trappers, but poachers, who were violating the game laws and planning to annihilate the whole beaver colony by fencing in its brush pile.

The Boy realized now that the situation was a delicate if not a dangerous one. For an instant he thought of going back to camp for help; but one of the men was on his knees, fixing the stakes, and the other was already chopping what appeared to be the last hole. Delay might mean the death of several of his precious beavers. Indignation and compassion together urged him on, and his young face hardened in unaccustomed lines.

Walking out upon the snow a little way, he halted, at a distance of perhaps thirty paces from the poachers. At the sound of his snowshoes the two men looked up scowling and apprehensive; and the kneeling one sprang to his feet. They wanted no witnesses of their illegal work.

"Good morning," said the Boy politely.

At the sound of his soft young voice, the sight of his slender figure and youthful face, their apprehensions vanished; but not their anger at being discovered.

"Mornin'!" growled one, in a surly voice; while the other never opened his mouth. Then they looked at each other with meaning question in their eyes. How were they going to keep this unwelcome visitor from betraying them?

"I'm going to ask you," said the Boy sweetly, "to be so kind as to stop trapping on this pond. Of course you didn't know it, but this is my pond, and there is no trapping allowed on it. It is reserved, you know; and I don't want a single one of my beavers killed."

The man with the axe scowled fiercely and said nothing. But the other, the one who had been driving the stakes, laughed in harsh derision.

"You don't, hey, sonny?" he answered. "Well, you just wait an' watch us. We'll show ye whose beaver they be!" And turning his back in scorn of his interlocutor's youth, he knelt down again to drive another stake. The man who had not spoken, however, stood leaning on his axe, eying the Boy with an ugly expression of menace.

The Boy's usually quiet blood was now pounding and tingling with anger. His alert eyes had measured the whole situation, and noted that the men had no firearms but their rifles, which were leaning against a tree on the shore fully fifty yards behind them.

"Stop!" he cried, with so confident a tone of authority that the kneeling man looked up, though with a sneer on his face. "Unless you go away from this pond at once, I'll get the men from the camp, and they'll make you go. They'll not be so polite as I am. You're just poachers, anyway. And the boys will like as not just run you clean out of the country. Will you do as I ask you, or shall I go and get them?"

The man with the axe spat out some French curse which the Boy didn't understand very clearly. But the man at the stakes jumped up again with a dangerous grin.

"You'll stay right where you are, sonny, till we're done with you," he snarled. "You understand? You're a-goin' to git hurt ef ye gits in our way any! See?"

The Boy was now in a white rage; but he kept his wits cool and his eyes watchful. He realized at this moment that he was in great danger; but, his mettle being sound, this only made him the more resolute.

"All right. You've decided!" he said slowly. "We'll see what the boys will have to say about it."

As he spoke he made a movement as if to turn, but without taking his eyes from the enemy. The movement just served to swing his little Winchester into a readier position.

At his first move the man with the axe took a step forward, and swung up his axe with a peculiar gesture which the Boy understood. He had seen the woodsmen throw their axes. He knew well their quickness and their deadly precision. But quickness and precision with the little Winchester were his own especial pride,--and, after all, he had not turned any further than was just right for a good shot. Even as the axe was on the verge of leaving the poacher's hand, the rifle cracked sharply. The poacher yelled a curse, and his arm dropped. The axe flew wide, landing nowhere near its aim. On the instant both the half-breeds turned, and raced for their rifles on the shore.

"Stop, or I'll shoot you both!" shouted the Boy, now with embarrassment added to his wrath. In their wild fury at being so balked by a boy, both men trusted to his missing his aim--or to the hope that his gun was not a repeater. They ignored his command, and rushed on. The Boy was just going to shoot again, aiming at their legs; when, to his amazement and inconceivable relief, out from behind the tree where the poachers' rifles leaned, came Jabe.

Snatching up one of the guns, he echoed the Boy's command.

"Stop right there!" he ordered curtly. "An' up with your hands, too! Mebbe youse kin fling a knife slick ez ye kin an axe."

The half-breeds stood like stones. One held up both hands; but the other only held up his left, his right being helpless. They knew there was nothing to say. They were fairly caught. They were poaching. The tall lumberman had seen the axe flung. Their case was a black one; and any attempt to explain could do no less than make it worse. They did not even dare to look at each other, but kept their narrow, beady eyes fixed on Jabe's face.

The Boy came swiftly to Jabe's side.

"Neat shot!" said the woodsman; but the note of astonished admiration in his tone was the most thrilling compliment the Boy had ever received.

"What are you going to do with them, Jabe?" he inquired, mildly.

"That's fer you to say! They're yourn!" answered Jabe, keeping his eyes on the prisoners.

The Boy looked the two culprits over carefully, with his calm, boyish gaze. He was overwhelmingly elated, but would have died rather than show it. His air was that of one who is quite used to capturing two outlaws,--and having axes hurled at his head,--and putting bullets through men's shoulders. He could not help feeling sorry for the man with the bullet through his shoulder.

"Well, Jabe," he said presently, "we can't let them go with their guns, because they're such sneaking brutes, they'd shoot us from behind a tree. And we can't let them go without their guns, because we can't be sure they wouldn't starve before they got to their own homes. And we don't want to take them into camp, for the fellows would probably treat them as they deserve,--and I don't want them to get anything so bad as that!"

"Maybe it might be better not to let the hands git hold of 'em!" agreed Jabe. "They'd be rough!"

A gleam of hope came into the prisoners' eyes. The unwounded one spoke. And he had the perspicacity to address himself to the Boy rather than to Jabe, thereby conciliating the Boy appreciably.

"Let us go!" he petitioned, choking down his rage. "We'll swear to quit, right now an' fer good; an' not to try to git back at yez!"

"Ye'll have to leave yer guns!" said Jabe sternly.

"They're the only guns we got; an' they're our livin', fer the winter!" protested the half-breed, still looking at the Boy.

"If we take away their guns, what's the good of making them swear?" demanded the Boy, stepping up and gazing into their eyes. "No, I reckon if they give their oath, they'll stick to it. Where's your camp, men?"

"Over yonder, about three mile!" answered the spokesman, nodding toward the northeast.

"If we give you back your guns," went on the Boy gently, "will you both give us your oath to clear right out of this country altogether, and not trap at all this side of the line? And will you take oath, also, that you will never, in any way, try to get even with either him or me for having downed you this way?"

"Sartain!" responded the spokesman, with obvious sincerity. "I'll swear to all that! An' I won't never want to git even, if you use us so gentlemanlike!"

"And will you swear, too?" inquired the Boy, turning to the silent one who had thrown the axe at him. The fellow glared at him defiantly for a moment, then glanced at his wounded arm, which hung limp at his side. At last he answered with a sullen growl:

"Yes, I'll swear! Got to! Curse you!"

"Good!" said the Boy. "That's the best way for all of us. Jabe, will you take their oaths. You know how better than I do!"

"All right!" responded the latter, shrugging his shoulders in a way which said--"it's your idee, not mine!" Then he proceeded to bind each man separately by an oath which left no loophole, and which was sealed by all that their souls held sacred. This done, he handed back the rifles,--and the two poachers, without a word, turned their backs and made off at a swift lope straight up the open pond. The Boy and Jabe watched them till they vanished among the trees. Then, with a shy little laugh, the Boy picked up the axe which had been hurled at his head.

"I'm glad he left me this," he murmured, "to kind of remember him by!"

"The sneakin' skunk!" growled Jabe. "If I'd had my way, it'd be the penitentiary for the both of 'em!"

That evening, when the whole story was told, the woodsmen were indignant, for a time, because the half-breeds had been let go; but at last they gave heed to Jabe's representations, and acknowledged that the Boy's plan had saved a "sight of bother." To guard against future difficulties, however, they took a big piece of smooth board, and painted the following sign, to be nailed up on a conspicuous tree beside the pond.

NOTICE

THIS IS BOY'S POND. NO TRAPPING HERE. IF ANYBODY WANTS TO SAY, WHY NOT? LAWLER'S CAMP WILL LET HIM KNOW.

THE WHITE-SLASHED BULL

HER back crushed beneath the massive weight of a "deadfall," the mother moose lay slowly sobbing her life out on the sweet spring air. The villainous log, weighted cunningly with rocks, had caught her just above the withers, bearing her forward so that her forelegs were doubled under her, and her neck outstretched so that she could not lift her muzzle from the wet moss. Though her eyes were already glazing, and her nostrils full of a blown and blood-streaked froth, from time to time she would struggle desperately to raise her head, for she yearned to lick the sprawling, wobbling legs of the ungainly calf which stood close beside her, bewildered because she would not rise and suckle him.

The dying animal lay in the middle of the trail, which was an old, half-obliterated logger's road, running straight east into the glow of the spring sunrise. The young birches and poplars, filmed with the first of the green, crowded close upon the trail, with, here and there, a rose-blooming maple, here and there, a sombre, black-green hemlock, towering over the thick second growth. The early air was fresh, but soft; fragrant with the breath of opening buds. Faint mists streamed up into the sunlight along the mossy line of the trail, and the only sounds breaking the silence of the wilderness were the sweetly plaintive calls of two rain-birds, answering each other slowly over the treetops. Everything in the scene--the tenderness of the colour and the air, the responses of the mating birds, the hope and the expectancy of all the waking world--seemed piteously at variance with the anguish of the stricken mother and her young, down there in the solitude of the trail.

Presently, in the undergrowth beside the trail, a few paces beyond the deadfall, a twig snapped sharply. Admonished by that experience of a thousand ancestral generations which is instinct, the calf lifted his big awkward ears apprehensively, and with a shiver drew closer to his mother's crushed body. A moment later a gaunt black bear thrust his head and shoulders forth from the undergrowth, and surveyed the scene with savage, but shrewd, little eyes. He was hungry, and to his palate no other delicacy the spring wilderness could ever afford was equal to a young moose calf. But the situation gave him pause. The mother moose was evidently in a trap; and the bear was wary of all traps. He sank back into the undergrowth, and crept noiselessly nearer to reconnoitre. In his suspicious eyes even a calf might be dangerous to tamper with, under such unusual conditions as these. As he vanished the calf shuddered violently, and tried to climb upon his mother's mangled body.

In a few seconds the bear's head appeared again, close by the base of the deadfall. With crafty nose he sniffed at the great timber which held the moose cow down. The calf was now almost within reach of the deadly sweep of his paw; but the man-smell was strong on the deadfall, and the bear was still suspicious. While he hesitated, from behind a bend in the trail came a sound of footsteps. The bear knew the sound. A man was coming. Yes, certainly there was some trick about it. With a grunt of indignant disgust he shrank back again into the thicket and fled stealthily from so dangerous a neighbourhood. Hungry as he was, he had no wish to try conclusions with man.

The woodsman came striding down the trail hurriedly, rounded the turn, and stopped abruptly. He understood at a glance the evil work of the game poachers. With indignant pity, he stepped forward and drew a merciful knife across the throat of the suffering beast. The calf shrank away and stood staring at him anxiously, wavering between terror and trust.

For a moment or two the man hesitated. Of one thing he was certain: the poachers who had set the deadfall must not profit by their success. Moreover, fresh moose-meat would not be unappreciated in his backwoods cabin. He turned and retraced his steps at a run, fearing lest some hungry spring marauders should arrive in his absence. And the calf, more than ever terrified by his mother's unresponsiveness, stared after him uneasily as he vanished.

For half an hour nothing happened. The early chill passed from the air, a comforting warmth glowed down the trail, the two rain-birds kept whistling to each other their long, persuasive, melancholy call, and the calf stood motionless, waiting, with the patience of the wild, for he knew not what. Then there came a clanking of chains, a trampling of heavy feet, and around the turn appeared the man again, with a pair of big brown horses harnessed to a drag-sled. The calf backed away as the man approached, and watched with dull wonder as the great log was rolled aside and his mother's limp, crushed form was hoisted laboriously upon the sled. This accomplished, the man turned and came to him gently, with hand outstretched. To run away would have been to run away from the shelter of his mother's presence; so, with a snort of apprehension, he submitted to being stroked and rubbed about the ears and neck and throat. The sensation was curiously comforting, and suddenly his fear vanished. With his long, mobile muzzle he began to tug appealingly at a convenient fold of the man's woollen sleeve. Smiling complacently at this sign of confidence, the man left him, and started the team at a slow walk up the trail. With a hoarse bleat of alarm, thinking he was about to be deserted, the calf followed after the sled, his long legs wobbling awkwardly.

From the first moment that she set eyes upon him, shambling awkwardly into the yard at her husband's heels, Jabe Smith's wife was inhospitable toward the ungainly youngling of the wild. She declared that he would take all the milk. And he did. For the next two months she was unable to make any butter, and her opinions on the subject were expressed without reserve. But Jabe was inflexible, in his taciturn, backwoods way, and the calf, till he was old enough to pasture, got all the milk he wanted. He grew and throve so astonishingly that Jabe began to wonder if there was not some mistake in the scheme of things, making cows' milk the proper nutriment for moose calves. By autumn the youngster was so big and sleek that he might almost have passed for a yearling.

Jabe Smith, lumberman, pioneer and guide, loved all animals, even those which in the fierce joy of the hunt he loved to kill. The young moose bull, however, was his peculiar favourite--partly, perhaps, because of Mrs. Smith's relentless hostility to it. And the ungainly youngster repaid his love with a devotion that promised to become embarrassing. All around the farm he was for ever at his heels, like a dog; and if, by any chance, he became separated from his idol, he would make for him in a straight line, regardless of currant bushes, bean rows, cabbage patches or clothes-lines. This strenuous directness did not further endear him to Mrs. Smith. That good lady used to lie awake at night, angrily devising schemes for getting rid of the "ugly brute." These schemes of vengeance were such a safety-valve to her injured feelings that she would at last make up her mind to content herself with "takin' it out on the hide o' the critter" next day, with a sound hickory stick. When next day came, however, and she went out to milk, the youngster would shamble up to greet her with such amiable trust in his eyes that her wrath would be, for the moment, disarmed, and her fell purpose would fritter out in a futile "Scat, you brute!" Then she would condone her weakness by thinking of what she would do to the animal "some day."

That "some day," as luck would have it, came rather sooner than she expected. From the first, the little moose had evinced a determination to take up his abode in the kitchen, in his dread of being separated from Jabe. Being a just man, Jabe had conceded at once that his wife should have the choosing of her kitchen guests; and, to avoid complications, he had rigged up a hinged bar across the kitchen doorway, so that the door could safely stand open. When the little bull was not at Jabe's heels, and did not know where to find him, his favourite attitude was standing in front of the kitchen door, his long nose thrust in as far as the bar would permit, his long ears waving hopefully, his eyes intently on the mysterious operations of Mrs. Jabe's housework. Though she would not have acknowledged it for worlds, even to her inmost heart, the good woman took much satisfaction out of that awkward, patient presence in the doorway. When things went wrong with her, in that perverse way so trying to the careful housewife, she could ease her feelings wonderfully by expressing them without reserve to the young moose, who never looked amused or attempted to answer back.

But one day, as it chanced, her feelings claimed a more violent easement--

and got it. She was scrubbing the kitchen floor. Just in the doorway stood the scrubbing-pail, full of dirty suds. On a chair close by stood a dish of eggs. The moose calf was nowhere in sight, and the bar was down. Tired and hot, she got up from her aching knees and went over to the stove to see if the pot was boiling, ready to make fresh suds.

At this moment the young bull, who had been searching in vain all over the farm for Jabe, came up to the door with a silent, shambling rush. The bar was down. Surely, then, Jabe was inside! Overjoyed at the opportunity he lurched his long legs over the threshold. Instantly his great, loose hoofs slid on the slippery floor, and he came down sprawling, striking the pail of dirty suds as he fell. With a seething souse the slops went abroad, all over the floor. At the same time the bouncing pail struck the chair, turned it over, and sent the dish of eggs crashing in every direction.

For one second Mrs. Jabe stared rigidly at the mess of eggs, suds and broken china, at the startled calf struggling to his feet. Then, with a hysterical scream, she turned, snatched the boiling pot from the stove, and hurled it blindly at the author of all mischief.

Happily for the blunderer, Mrs. Jabe's rage was so unbridled that she really tried to hit the object of it. Therefore, she missed. The pot went crashing through the leg of a table and shivered to atoms against the log wall, contributing its full share to the discouraging mess on the floor. But, as it whirled past, a great wedge of the boiling water leaped out over the rim, flew off at a tangent, and caught the floundering calf full in the side, in a long flare down from the tip of the left shoulder. The scalding fluid seemed to cling in the short, fine hair almost like an oil. With a loud bleat of pain the calf shot to his feet and went galloping around the yard. Mrs. Jabe rushed to the door, and stared at him wide-eyed. In a moment her senses came back to her, and she realized what a hideous thing she had done. Next she remembered Jabe-- and what he would think of it!

Then, indeed, her conscience awoke in earnest, and a wholesome dread enlivened her remorse. Forgetting altogether the state of her kitchen, she rushed through the slop to the flour-barrel. Flour, she had always heard, was the thing for burns and scalds. The pesky calf should be treated right, if it took the whole barrel. Scooping up an extravagant dishpanful of the white, powdery stuff, and recklessly spilling a lot of it to add to the mixture on the floor, she rushed out into the yard to apply her treatment, and, if possible, poultice her conscience.

The young moose, anguished and bewildered, had at last taken refuge in the darkest corner of the stable. As Mrs. Jabe approached with her pan of flour, he stood staring and shaking, but made no effort to avoid her, which touched the over-impetuous dame to a fresh pang of penitence. She did not know that the stupid youngster had quite failed to associate her in any way with his suffering. It was only the pot--the big, black thing which had so inexplicably come bounding at him--that he blamed. From Mrs. Jabe's hands he expected some kind of consolation.

In the gloom of the stall Mrs. Jabe could not see the extent of the calf's injury. "Mebbe the water wasn't quite bilin'!" she murmured hopefully, coaxing and dragging the youngster forth into the light. The hope, however, proved vain as brief. In a long streak down behind the shoulder the hair was already slipping off.

"Sarved ye right!" she grumbled remorsefully, as with gentle fingers she began sifting the flour up and down over the wound. The light stuff seemed to soothe the anguish for the moment, and the sufferer stood quite still till the scald was thoroughly covered with a tenacious white cake. Then a fresh and fiercer pang seized the wound. With a bleat he tore himself away, and rushed off, tail in air, across the stump-pasture and into the woods.

"Mebbe he won't come back, and then Jabe won't never need to know!" soliloquized Mrs. Jabe, returning to clean up her kitchen.

The sufferer returned, however, early in the afternoon, and was in his customary attitude before the door when Jabe, a little later, came back also. The long white slash down his favourite's side caught the woodsman's eye at once. He looked at it critically, touched the flour with tentative finger-tips, then turned on his wife a look of poignant interrogation. But Mrs. Jabe was ready for him. Her nerve had recovered. The fact that her victim showed no fear of her had gradually reassured her. What Jabe didn't know would never hurt him, she mused.

"Yes, yer pesky brat come stumblin' into the kitchen when the bar was down, a-lookin' for ye. An' he upset the bilin' water I was goin' to scrub with, an' broke the pot. An' I've got to have a new pot right off, Jabe Smith--mind that!"

"Scalded himself pretty bad!" remarked Jabe. "Poor little beggar!"

"I done the best I know'd how fer him!" said his wife with an injured air. "Wasted most a quart o' good flour on his worthless hide! Wish't he'd broke his neck 'stead of the only pot I got that's big enough to bile the pig's feed in!"

"Well, you done jest about right, I reckon, Mandy," replied Jabe, ashamed of his suspicions. "I'll go in to the Cross Roads an' git ye a new pot to-morrer, an' some tar for the scald. The tar'll be better'n flour, an' keep the flies off."

"I s'pose some men ain't got nothin' better to do than be doctorin' up a fool moose calf!" assented Mrs. Jabe promptly, with a snort of censorious resignation.

Whether because the flour and the tar had virtues, or because the clean flesh of the wild kindreds makes all haste to purge itself of ills, it was not long before the scald was perfectly healed. But the reminder of it remained ineffaceable--a long, white slash down across the brown hide of the young bull, from the tip of the left fore shoulder.

Throughout the winter the young moose contentedly occupied the cow-stable, with the two cows and the yoke of red oxen. He throve on the fare Jabe provided for him--good meadow hay with armfuls of "browse" cut from the birch, poplar and cherry thickets. Jabe trained him to haul a pung, finding him slower to learn than a horse, but making up for his dulness by his docility. He had to be driven with a snaffle, refusing absolutely to admit a bit between his teeth; and, with the best good-will in the world, he could never be taught to allow for the pung or sled to which he was harnessed. If left alone for a moment he would walk over fences with it, or through the most tangled thickets, if thereby seemed the most direct way to reach Jabe; and once, when Jabe, vaingloriously and at great speed, drove him in to the Cross Roads, he smashed the vehicle to kindling-wood in the amiable determination to follow his master into the Cross Roads store. On this occasion also he made himself respected, but unpopular, by killing, with one lightning stroke of a great fore hoof, a huge mongrel mastiff belonging to the storekeeper. The mastiff had sprung out at him wantonly, resenting his peculiar appearance. But the storekeeper had been so aggrieved that Jabe had felt constrained to mollify him with a five-dollar bill. He decided, therefore, that his favourite's value was as a luxury, rather than a utility; and the young bull was put no more to the practices of a horse. Jabe had driven a bull moose in harness, and all the settlement could swear to it. The glory was all his.

By early summer the young bull was a tremendous, long-legged, high-shouldered beast, so big, so awkward, so friendly, and so sure of everybody's good-will that everybody but Jabe was terribly afraid of him. He had no conception of the purposes of a fence; and he could not be taught that a garden was not meant for him to lie down in. As the summer advanced, and the young bull's stature with it, Jabe Smith began to realize that his favourite was an expensive and sometimes embarrassing luxury. Nevertheless, when September brought budding spikes of horns and a strange new restlessness to the stalwart youngster, and the first full moon of October lured him one night away from the farm on a quest which he could but blindly follow, Jabe was inconsolable.

"He ain't no more'n a calf yet, big as he is!" fretted Jabe. "He'll be gittin' himself shot, the fool. Or mebbe some old bull'll be after givin' him a lickin' fer interferin', and he'll come home to us!"

To which his wife retorted with calm superiority: "Ye're a bigger fool'n even I took ye fer, Jabe Smith."

But the young bull did not come back that winter, nor the following summer, nor the next year, nor the next. Neither did any Indian or hunter or lumberman have anything to report as to a bull moose of great stature, with a long white slash down his side. Either his quest had carried him far to other and alien ranges, or some fatal mischance of the wild had overtaken his inexperience. The latter was Jabe's belief, and he concluded that his ungainly favourite had too soon taken the long trail for the Red Men's land of ghosts.

Though Jabe Smith was primarily a lumberman and backwoods farmer, he was also a hunter's guide, so expert that his services in this direction were not to be obtained without very special inducement. At "calling" moose he was acknowledged to have no rival. When he laid his grimly-humourous lips to the long tube of birch-bark, which is the "caller's" instrument of illusion, there would come from it a strange sound, great and grotesque, harsh yet appealing, rude yet subtle, and mysterious as if the uncomprehended wilderness had itself found voice. Old hunters, wise in all woodcraft, had been deceived by the sound--and much more easily the impetuous bull, waiting, high-antlered and eager, for the love-call of his mate to summon him down the shore of the still and moon-tranced lake.

When a certain Famous Hunter, whose heart took pride in horns and heads and hides--the trophies won by his unerring rifle in all four corners of earth-- found his way at last to the tumbled wilderness that lies about the headwaters of the Quah Davic, it was naturally one of the great New Brunswick moose that he was after. Nothing but the noblest antlers that New Brunswick forests bred could seem to him worthy of a place on those walls of his, whence the surly front of a musk-ox of the Barren Grounds glared stolid defiance to the snarl of an Orinoco jaguar, and the black, colossal head of a

Kadiak bear was eyed derisively by the monstrous and malignant mask of a two-horned rhinoceros. With such a quest upon him, the Famous Hunter came, and naturally sought the guidance of Jabe Smith, whom he lured from the tamer distractions of a "timber cruise" by double pay and the pledge of an extravagant bonus if the quest should be successful.

The lake, lying low between its wooded hills, was like a glimmering mirror in the misty October twilight when Jabe and the Famous Hunter crept stealthily down to it. In a dense covert beside the water's edge they hid themselves. Beside them stretched the open ribbon of a narrow water-meadow, through which a slim brook, tinkling faintly over its pebbles, slipped out into the stillness. Just beyond the mouth of the brook a low, bare spit of sand jutted forth darkly upon the pale surface of the lake.

It was not until the moon appeared--a red, ominous segment of a disk--over the black and rugged ridge of the hills across the lake, that Jabe began to call. Three times he set the hollow birch-bark to his mouth, and sent the hoarse, appealing summons echoing over the water. And the man, crouching invisible in the thick shadow beside him, felt a thrill in his nerves, a prickling in his cheeks, at that mysterious cry, which seemed to him to have something almost of menace in its lure. Even so, he thought, might Pan have summoned his followers, shaggy and dangerous, yet half divine, to some symbolic revel.

The call evoked no answer of any kind. Jabe waited till the moon, still red and distorted, had risen almost clear of the ridge. Then he called again, and yet again, and again waited. From straight across the strangely-shadowed water came a sudden sharp crashing of underbrush, as if some one had fallen to beating the bushes furiously with sticks.

"That's him!" whispered Jabe. "An' he's a big one, sure!"

The words were not yet out of his mouth when there arose a most startling commotion in the thicket close behind them, and both men swung around like lightning, jerking up their rifles. At the same instant came an elusive whiff of pungency on the chill.

"Pooh! only a bear!" muttered Jabe, as the commotion retreated in haste.

"Why, he was close upon us!" remarked the visitor. "I could have poked him with my gun! Had he any special business with us, do you suppose?"

"Took me for a cow moose, an' was jest a-goin' to swipe me!" answered Jabe, rather elated at the compliment which the bear had paid to his counterfeit.

The Famous Hunter drew a breath of profound satisfaction.

"I'll be hanged," he whispered, "if your amiable New Brunswick backwoods can't get up a thrill quite worthy of the African jungle!"

"St!" admonished Jabe. "He's a-comin'. An' mad, too! Thinks that racket was another bull, gittin' ahead of 'im. Don't ye breathe now, no more!" And raising the long bark, he called through it again, this time more softly, more enticingly, but always with that indescribable wildness, shyness and roughness rasping strangely through the note. The hurried approach of the bull could be followed clearly around the head of the lake. It stopped, and Jabe called again. In a minute or two there came a brief, explosive, grunting reply--this time from a point much nearer. The great bull had stopped his crashing progress and was slipping his vast, impetuous bulk through the underbrush as noiselessly as a weasel. The stillness was so perfect after that one echoing response that the Famous Hunter turned a look of interrogation upon Jabe's shadowy face. The latter breathed almost inaudibly: "He's a-comin'. He's nigh here!" And the hunter clutched his rifle with that fine, final thrill of unparalleled anticipation.

The moon was now well up, clear of the treetops and the discolouring mists, hanging round and honey-yellow over the hump of the ridge. The magic of the night deepened swiftly. The sandspit and the little water-meadow stood forth unshadowed in the spectral glare. Far out in the shine of the lake a fish jumped, splashing sharply. Then a twig snapped in the dense growth beyond the water-meadow. Jabe furtively lifted the bark, and mumbled in it caressingly. The next moment--so suddenly and silently that it seemed as if he had taken instant shape in the moonlight--appeared a gigantic moose, standing in the meadow, his head held high, his nostrils sniffing arrogant inquiry. The broadly-palmated antlers crowning his mighty head were of a spread and symmetry such as Jabe had never even imagined.

Almost imperceptibly the Hunter raised his rifle--a slender shadow moving in paler shadows. The great bull, gazing about expectantly for the mate who had called, stood superb and indomitable, ghost-gray in the moonlight, a mark no tyro could miss. A cherry branch intervened, obscuring the foresight of the Hunter's rifle. The Hunter shifted his position furtively. His crooked finger was just about to tighten on the trigger. At this moment, when the very night hung stiller as if with a sense of crisis, the giant bull turned, exposing his left flank to the full glare of the moonlight. Something gleamed silver down his side, as if it were a shining belt thrown across his shoulder.

With a sort of hiss from between his teeth Jabe shot out his long arm and knocked up the barrel of the rifle. In the same instant the Hunter's finger had closed on the trigger. The report rang out, shattering the night; the bullet whined away high over the treetops, and the great bull, springing at one bound far back into the thickets, vanished like an hallucination.

Jabe stood forth into the open, his gaunt face working with suppressed excitement. The Hunter followed, speechless for a moment between amazement, wrath and disappointment. At last he found voice, and quite forgot his wonted courtesy.

"D--n you!" he stammered. "What do you mean by that? What in----"

But Jabe, suddenly calm, turned and eyed him with a steadying gaze.

"Quit all that, now!" he retorted crisply. "I knowed jest what I was doin'! I knowed that bull when he were a leetle, awkward staggerer. I brung him up on a bottle; an' I loved him. He skun out four years ago. I'd most ruther 'ave seen you shot than that ther' bull, I tell ye!"

The Famous Hunter looked sour; but he was beginning to understand the situation, and his anger died down. As he considered, Jabe, too, began to see the other side of the situation.

"I'm right sorry to disapp'int ye so!" he went on apologetically. "We'll hev to call off this deal atween you an' me, I reckon. An' there ain't goin' to be no more shooting over this range, if I kin help it--an' I guess I kin!--till I kin git that ther' white-slashed bull drove away back over on to the Upsalquitch, where the hunters won't fall foul of him! But I'll git ye another guide, jest as good as me, or better, what ain't got no particular friends runnin' loose in the woods to bother 'im. An' I'll send ye 'way down on to the Sevogle, where ther's as big heads to be shot as ever have been. I can't do more."

"Yes, you can!" declared the Famous Hunter, who had quite recovered his self-possession.

"What is it?" asked Jabe doubtfully.

"You can pardon me for losing my temper and swearing at you!" answered the Famous Hunter, holding out his hand. "I'm glad I didn't knock over your magnificent friend. It's good for the breed that he got off. But you'll have to find me something peculiarly special now, down on that Sevogle."

WHEN THE BLUEBERRIES ARE RIPE

THE steep, rounded, rock-scarred face of Bald Mountain, for all its naked grimness, looked very cheerful in the last of the warm-coloured sunset. There were no trees; but every little hollow, every tiny plateau, every bit of slope that was not too steep for clinging roots to find hold, was clothed with a mat of blueberry bushes. The berries, of an opaque violet-blue tone (much more vivid and higher in key than the same berries can show when picked and brought to market) were so large and so thickly crowded as to almost hide the leaves. They gave the austere steeps of "Old Baldy" the effect of having been dyed with a wash of cobalt.

Far below, where the lonely wilderness valley was already forsaken by the sun, a flock of ducks could be seen, with long, outstretched necks rigid and short wings swiftly beating, lined out over a breadth of wild meadow. Above the lake which washed the foot of the mountain,--high above the water, but below the line of shadow creeping up the mountain's face,--a single fish-hawk circled slowly, waiting for the twilight coolness to bring the big trout to the surface to feed. The smooth water glimmered pallidly, and here and there a spreading, circular ripple showed that the hungry fish were beginning to rise.

Up in the flood of the sunset, the blueberries basked and glowed, some looking like gems, some like blossoms, according to the fall of the light. Around the shoulder of the mountain toward the east, where the direct rays of the sun could not reach, the light was yet abundant, but cool and tender,-- and here the vivid berries were beginning to lose their colour, as a curved moon, just rising over the far, ragged rim of the forest, touched them with phantom silver. Everywhere jutting rocks and sharp crevices broke the soft mantle of the blueberry thickets; and on the southerly slope, where sunset and moonrise mingled with intricate shadows, everything looked ghostlike and unreal. On the utmost summit of the mountain a rounded peak of white granite, smoothed by ages of storm, shone like a beacon.

The only berry-pickers that came to these high slopes of Bald Mountain were the wild kindreds, furred and feathered. Of them all, none were more enthusiastic and assiduous than the bears; and just now, climbing up eagerly from the darkening woods below, came an old she-bear with two half-grown cubs. They came up by easy paths, zigzagging past boulder and crevice, through the ghostly, noiseless contention of sunlight and moonlight. Now their moving shadows lay one way, now the other; and now their shadows were suddenly wiped out, as the two lights for a moment held an even balance. At length having reached a little plateau where the berries were particularly large and close-clustered, the old bear stopped, and they fell joyously to their feeding.

On these open heights there were no enemies to keep watch against, and there was no reason to be wary or silent. The bears fed noisily, therefore, stripping the plump fruit cleverly by the pawful, and munching with little, greedy grunts of delight. There was no other food quite so to their taste as these berries, unless, perhaps, a well-filled honey-comb. And this was their season for eating, eating, eating, all the time, in order to lay up abundant fat against the long severity of winter.

As the bushes about them were stripped of the best fruit, the shaggy feasters moved around the shoulder of the mountain from the gold of the sun into the silver of the moon. Soon the sunset had faded, and the moon had it all her own way except for a broad expanse of sea-green sky in the west, deepening through violet to a narrow streak of copper on the horizon. By this time the shadows, especially on the eastern slope, were very sharp and black, and the open spaces very white and radiant, with a strange transparency borrowed from that high, pure atmosphere.

It chanced that the little hollow on which the bears were just now revelling,--a hollow where the blueberries were unbelievably large and abundant--was bounded on its upper side, toward the steep, by a narrow and deep crevice. At one end of the cleft, from a rocky and shallow roothold, a gnarled birch grew slantingly. From its unusual situation, and from the fact that the bushes grew thick to its very edge, this crevice constituted nothing less than a most insidious trap.

One of the cubs, born with the instinct of caution, kept far away from the dangerous brink without having more than half realized that there was any danger there whatever. The other cub was one of those blundering fellows, to be found among the wild kindreds no less than among the kindreds of men, who only get caution hammered into them by experience. He saw a narrow break, indeed, between the berry patch and the bare steep above,--but what was a little crevice in a position like this, where it could not amount to anything? Had it been on the other side of the hollow, he would have feared a precipice, and would have been on his guard. But, as it was, he never gave the matter a second thought, because it did not look dangerous! He found the best berries growing very near the edge of the crevice; and in his satisfaction he turned his back to the height and settled himself solidly upon his haunches to enjoy them. As he did so the bushes gave way behind him, he pitched abruptly backwards, and vanished with a squeal of terror into the narrow cleft of darkness.

The crevice was perhaps twelve feet deep, and from five to eight in width all the way to the bottom. The bottom held a layer of earth and dead leaves, which served to ease the cub's fall; but when he landed the wind was so bumped out of him that for a minute or two he could not utter a sound. As soon as he recovered his voice, however, he began to squeal and whine piteously for his mother.

The old bear, at the sound of his cry as he fell, had rushed so hastily to his aid that she barely escaped falling in after him. Checking herself just in time, by digging all her mighty claws into the roots of the blueberries, she crouched at the brink, thrust her head as far over as she could, and peered down with anxious cries. But when the cub's voice came back to her from the darkness she knew he was not killed, and she also knew that he was very near,--and her whinings changed at once to a guttural murmur that must have been intended for encouragement. The other cub, meanwhile, had come lumbering up with ears wisely cocked, taken a very hasty and careful glance over the edge, and returned to his blueberries with an air of disapproval. It was as if he said he always knew that blundering brother of his would get himself into trouble.

For some minutes the old bear crouched where she was, straining her eyes to make out the form of her little one. Becoming accustomed to the gloom at last, she could discern him. She could see that he was moving about, and standing on his hind legs, and striving valiantly to claw his way up the perpendicular surface of smooth rock. She began to reach downwards first one big forepaw and then the other, testing the rock beneath her for some ledge or crack that might give her foothold by which to climb down to his aid. Finding none, she again set up her uneasy whining, and moved slowly along the brink, trying every inch of the way for some place rough enough to give her strong claws a chance to take hold. In the full, unclouded light of the white moon she was a pathetic figure, bending and crouching and straining, and reaching down longingly, then stopping to listen to the complaints of pain and terror that came up out of the dark.

At last she came to the end of the crevice where grew the solitary birch tree,--the frightened captive following exactly below her and stretching up toward her against the rock. At this point, close beside the tree, some roots and tough turf overhung the edge, and the old bear's paws detected a roughness on the face of the rock just below. This was enough for her brave and devoted heart. She turned around and let her hind quarters carefully over the brink, intending to climb down backwards as bears do. But beyond the first unevenness there was absolutely nothing that her claws could take hold of. Her great body was half way over, when she felt herself on the point of falling. Making a sudden startled effort to recover herself, she clutched desperately at the trunk of the birch tree with one arm, at the roots of the berry-bushes with the other,--and just managed to regain the level.

For herself, this mighty effort was just enough. But for the birch-tree it was just too much. The shallow earth by which it held gave way; and the next moment, with a clatter of loosened stones and a swish of leafy branches, it crashed majestically down into the crevice, closing one end of it with a mass of boughs and foliage, and once more frightening the imprisoned cub almost out of his senses.

At the first sound of this cataclysm, at the first rattle of loose earth about his ears, the cub had bounced madly to the other end of the crevice, where he crouched, whimpering. The old bear, too, was daunted for some seconds; but then, seeing that the cub was not hurt, she was quick to perceive the advantage of the accident. Standing at the upturned roots of the tree, she called eagerly and encouragingly to the cub, pointing out the path of escape thus offered to him. For some minutes he was too terrified to approach. At last she set her own weight on the trunk, testing it, and prepared to climb down and lead him out. At this, however, the youngster's nerve revived. With a joyful and understanding squeal, he rushed forward, sprawled and clawed his way over the tangle of branches, gained the firm trunk,--and presently found himself again beside his mother among the pleasant, moonlit berry-bushes. Here he was fondled and nosed and licked and nursed by the delighted mother, till his bruised little body forgot its hurts and his shaken little heart its fears. His cautious brother, too, came up with a wise look and sniffed at him patronizingly; but went away again with his nose in the air, as if to say that here was much fuss being made over a very small matter.

THE GLUTTON OF THE GREAT SNOW

I

NORTHWARD interminably, and beneath a whitish, desolate sky, stretched the white, empty leagues of snow, unbroken by rock or tree or hill, to the straight, menacing horizon. Green-black, and splotched with snow that clung here and there upon their branches, along the southward limits of the barren crowded down the serried ranks of the ancient fir forest. Endlessly baffled, but endlessly unconquered, the hosts of the firs thrust out their grim spire-topped vanguards, at intervals, into the hostile vacancy of the barren. Between these dark vanguards, long, silent aisles of whiteness led back and gently upward into the heart of the forest.

Out across one of these pale corridors of silence came moving very deliberately a dark, squat shape with blunt muzzle close to the snow. Its keen, fierce eyes and keener nostrils were scrutinizing the white surface for the scent or trail of some other forest wanderer. Conscious of power, in spite of its comparatively small stature--much less than that of wolf or lynx, or even of the fox--it made no effort to conceal its movements, disguise its track or keep watch for possible enemies. Stronger than any other beast of thrice its size, as cunning as the wisest of the foxes, and of a dogged, savage temper well known to all the kindred of the wild, it seemed to feel secure from ill-considered interference.

Less than three feet in length, but of peculiarly massive build, this dark, ominous-looking animal walked flat-footed, like a bear, and with a surly heaviness worthy of a bear's stature. Its fur, coarse and long, was of a sooty gray-brown, streaked coarsely down each flank with a broad yellowish splash meeting over the hind quarters. Its powerful, heavy-clawed feet were black. Its short muzzle and massive jaw, and its broad face up to just above the eyes, where the fur came down thickly, were black also. The eyes themselves, peering out beneath overhanging brows, gleamed with a mixture of sullen intelligence and implacable savagery. In its slow, forbidding strength, and in its tameless reserve, which yet held the capacity for outbursts of ungovernable rage, this strange beast seemed to incarnate the very spirit of the bitter and indomitable North. Its name was various, for hunters called it sometimes wolverene, sometimes carcajou, but oftener "Glutton," or "Injun Devil."

Through the voiceless desolation the carcajou--it was a female--continued her leisurely way. Presently, just upon the edge of the forest-growth, she came upon the fresh track of a huge lynx. The prints of the lynx's great pads were several times broader than her own, but she stopped and began to examine them without the slightest trace of apprehension. For some reason best known to herself, she at length made up her mind to pursue the stranger's back trail, concerning herself rather with what he had been doing than with what he was about to do.

Plunging into the gloom of the firs, where the trail led over a snow-covered chaos of boulders and tangled windfalls, she came presently to a spot where the snow was disturbed and scratched. Her eyes sparkled greedily. There were spatters of blood about the place, and she realized that here the lynx had buried, for a future meal, the remnant of his kill.

Her keen nose speedily told her just where the treasure was hidden, and she fell to digging furiously with her short, powerful fore paws. It was a bitter and lean season, and the lynx, after eating his fill, had taken care to bury the remnant deep. The carcajou burrowed down till only the tip of her dingy tail was visible before she found the object of her search. It proved to be nothing but one hind quarter of a little blue fox. Angrily she dragged it forth and bolted it in a twinkling, crunching the slim bone between her powerful jaws. It was but a morsel to such a hunger as hers. Licking her chops, and passing her black paws hurriedly over her face, as a cat does, she forsook the trail of the lynx and wandered on deeper into the soundless gloom. Several rabbit-tracks she crossed, and here and there the dainty trail of a ptarmigan, or the small, sequential dots of a weasel's foot. But a single glance or passing twitch of her nostril told her these were all old, and she vouchsafed them no attention. It was not till she had gone perhaps a quarter of a mile through the fir-glooms that she came upon a trail which caused her to halt.

It was the one trail, this, among all the tracks that traversed the great snow, which could cause her a moment's perturbation. For the trail of the wolf-pack she had small concern--for the hungriest wolves could never climb a tree. But this was the broad snowshoe trail, which she knew was made by a creature even more crafty than herself. She glanced about keenly, peering under the trees--because one could never judge, merely by the direction of the trail, where one of those dangerous creatures was going. She stood almost erect on her haunches and sniffed the air for the slightest taint of danger. Then she sniffed at the tracks. The man-smell was strong upon them, and comparatively, but not dangerously, fresh. Reassured on this point, she decided to follow the man and find out what he was doing. It was only when she did not know what he was about that she so dreaded him. Given the opportunity to watch him unseen, she was willing enough to pit her cunning against his, and to rob him as audaciously as she would rob any of the wilderness kindreds.

Hunting over a wide range as she did, the carcajou was unaware till now that a man had come upon her range that winter. To her experience a man meant a hunter--and--trapper, with emphasis distinctly upon the trapper. The man's gun she feared--but his traps she feared not at all. Indeed, she regarded them rather with distinct favour, and was ready to profit by them at the first opportunity. Having only strength and cunning, but no speed to rely upon, she had learned that traps could catch all kinds of swift creatures, and hold them inexorably. She had learned, too, that there was usually a succession of traps and snares set along a man's trail. It was with some exciting expectation, now, that she applied herself to following this trail.

Within a short distance the track brought her to a patch of trampled snow, with tiny bits of frozen fish scattered about. She knew at once that somewhere in this disturbed area a trap was hidden, close to the surface. Stepping warily, in a circle, she picked up and devoured the smallest scraps. Near the centre lay a fragment of tempting size; but she cunningly guessed that close beside that morsel would be the hiding-place of the trap. Slowly she closed in upon it, her nose close to the snow, sniffing with cautious discrimination. Suddenly she stopped short. Through the snow she had detected the man-smell, and the smell of steel, mingling with the savour of the dried fish. Here, but a little to one side, she began to dig, and promptly uncovered a light chain. Following this she came presently to the trap itself, which she cautiously laid bare. Then, without misgiving, she ate the big piece of fish. Both her curiosity and her hunger, however, were still far from satisfied, so she again took up the trail.

The next trap she came to was an open snare--a noose of bright wire suspended near the head of a cunningly constructed alley of fir branches, leading up to the foot of a big hemlock. Just behind this noose, and hardly to be reached save through the noose, the bait had evidently been fixed. But the carcajou saw that some one little less cunning than herself had been before her. Such a snare would have caught the fierce, but rather stupid, lynx; but a fox had been the first arrival. She saw his tracks. He had carefully investigated the alley of fir branches from the outside. Then he had broken through it behind the noose, and safely made off with the bait. Rather contemptuously the old wolverene went on. She did not understand this kind of trap, so she discreetly refrained from meddling with it.

Fully a quarter mile she had to go before she came to another; but here she found things altogether different and more interesting. As she came softly around a great snow-draped boulder there was a snarl, a sharp rattle of steel, and a thud. She shrank back swiftly, just beyond reach of the claws of a big lynx. The lynx had been ahead of her in discovering the trap, and with the stupidity of his tribe had got caught in it. The inexorable steel jaws had him fast by the left fore leg. He had heard the almost soundless approach of the strange prowler, and, mad with pain and rage, had sprung to the attack without waiting to see the nature of his antagonist.

Keeping just beyond the range of his hampered leap, the carcajou now crept slowly around the raging and snarling captive, who kept pouncing at her in futile fury every other moment. Though his superior in sheer strength, she was much smaller and lighter than he, and less murderously armed for combat; and she dreaded the raking, eviscerating clutch of his terrible hinder claws. In defence of her burrow and her litter, she would have tackled him without hesitation; but her sharp teeth and bulldog jaw, however efficient, would not avail, in such a combat, to save her from getting ripped almost to ribbons. She was far too sagacious to enter upon any such struggle unnecessarily. Prowling slowly and tirelessly, without effort, around and around the excited prisoner, she trusted to wear him out and then take him at some deadly disadvantage.

Weighted with the trap, and not wise enough to refrain from wasting his strength in vain struggles, the lynx was strenuously playing his cunning antagonist's game, when a sound came floating on the still air which made them both instantly rigid. It was a long, thin, wavering cry that died off with indescribable melancholy in its cadence. The lynx crouched, with eyes dilating, and listened with terrible intentness. The carcajou, equally interested but not terrified, stood erect, ears, eyes and nose alike directed to finding out more about that ominous voice. Again and again it was repeated, swiftly coming nearer; and presently it resolved itself into a chorus of voices. The lynx made several convulsive bounds, wrenching desperately to free his imprisoned limb; then, recognizing the inevitable, he crouched again, shuddering but dangerous, his tufted ears flattened upon his back, his eyes flickering green, every tooth and claw bared for the last battle. But the carcajou merely stiffened up her fur, in a rage at the prospective interruption of her hunting. She knew well that the dreadful, melancholy cry was the voice of the wolf-pack. But the wolves were not on her trail, that she was sure of; and possibly they might pass at a harmless distance, and not discover her or her quarry.

The listeners were not kept long in suspense. The pack, as it chanced, was on the trail of a moose which, labouring heavily in the deep snow, had passed, at a distance of some thirty or forty yards, a few minutes before the carcajou's arrival. The wolves swept into view through the tall fir trunks--five in number, and running so close that a table-cloth might have covered them. They knew by the trail that the quarry must be near, and, urged on by the fierce thrust of their hunger, they were not looking to right or left. They were almost past, and the lynx was beginning to take heart again, when, out of the tail of his eye, the pack-leader detected something unusual on the snow near the foot of the big rock. One fair look explained it all to him. With an exultant yelp he turned, and the pack swept down upon the prisoner; while the carcajou, bursting with indignation, slipped up the nearest tree.

The captive was not abject, but game to the last tough fibre. All fangs and rending claws, with a screech and a bound he met the onslaught of the pack; and, for all the hideous handicap of that thing of iron on his leg, he gave a good account of himself. For a minute or two the wolves and their victim formed one yelling, yelping heap. When it disentangled itself, three of the wolves were badly torn, and one had the whole side of his face laid open. But in a few minutes there was nothing left of the unfortunate lynx but a few of the heavier bones--to which the pack might return later--and the scrap of fur and flesh that was held in the jaws of the trap.

As the carcajou saw her prospective meal disappearing, her rage became almost uncontrollable, and she crept down the tree-trunk as if she would fling herself upon the pack. The leader sprang at her, leaping as high as he could against the trunk; and she, barely out of reach of his clashing, bloody fangs, snapped back at him with a vicious growl, trying to catch the tip of his nose. Failing in this, she struck at him like lightning with her powerful claws, raking his muzzle so severely that he fell back with a startled yelp. A moment later the whole pack, their famine still unsatisfied, swept off again upon the trail of the moose. The carcajou came down, sniffed angrily at the clean bones which had been cracked for their marrow, then hurried off on the track of the wolves.

II

Meanwhile, it had chanced that the man on snowshoes, fetching a wide circle that would bring the end of his line of traps back nearly to his cabin, had come suddenly face to face with the fleeing moose. Worn out with the terror of his flight and the heart-breaking effort of floundering through the heavy snow--which was, nevertheless, hard enough, on the surface, to bear up his light-footed pursuers--the great beast was near his last gasp. At sight of the man before him, more to be dreaded even than the savage foe behind him, he snorted wildly and plunged off to one side. But the man, borne up upon his snowshoes, overtook him in a moment, and, suddenly stooping forward, drew his long hunting-knife across the gasping throat. The snow about grew crimson instantly, and the huge beast sank with a shudder.

The trapper knew that a moose so driven must have had enemies on its trail, and he knew also that no enemies but wolves, or another hunter, could have driven the moose to such a flight. There was no other hunter ranging within twenty miles of him. Therefore, it was wolves. He had no weapon with him but his knife and his light axe, because his rifle was apt to be a useless burden in winter, when he had always traps or pelts to carry. And it was rash for one man, without his gun, to rob a wolf-pack of its kill! But the trapper wanted fresh moose-meat. Hastily and skilfully he began to cut from the carcass the choicest portions of haunch and loin. He had no more than fairly got to work when the far-off cry of the pack sounded on his expectant ears. He laboured furiously as the voices drew nearer. The interruption of the lynx he understood, in a measure, by the noises that reached him; but when the pack came hot on the trail again he knew it was time to get away. He must retreat promptly, but not be seen retreating. Bearing with him such cuts as he had been able to secure, he made off in the direction of his cabin. But at a distance of about two hundred yards he stepped into a thicket at the base of a huge hemlock, and turned to see what the wolves would do when they found they had been forestalled. As he turned, the wolves appeared, and swept down upon the body of the moose. But within a couple of paces of it they stopped short, with a snarl of suspicion, and drew back hastily. The tracks and the scent of their arch-enemy, man, were all about the carcass. His handiwork--his clean cutting--was evident upon it. Their first impulse was toward caution. Suspecting a trap, they circled warily about the body. Then, reassured, their rage blazed up. Their own quarry had been killed before them, their own hunting insolently crossed. However, it was man, the ever-insolent overlord, who had done it. He had taken toll as he would, and withdrawn when he would. They did not quite dare to follow and seek vengeance. So in a few moments their wrath had simmered down; and they fell savagely upon the yet warm feast.

The trapper watched them from his hiding-place, not wishing to risk attracting their attention before they had quite gorged themselves. He knew there would be plenty of good meat left, even then; and that they would at length proceed to bury it for future use. Then he could dig it up again, take what remained clean and unmauled, and leave the rest to its lawful owners; and all without unnecessary trouble.

As he watched the banqueting pack, he was suddenly conscious of a movement in the branches of a fir a little beyond them. Then his quick eye, keener in discrimination than that of any wolf, detected the sturdy figure of a large wolverene making its way from tree to tree at a safe distance above the snow, intent upon the wolves. What one carcajou--"Glutton," he called it-- could hope, for all its cunning, to accomplish against five big timber-wolves, he could not imagine. Hating the "Glutton," as all trappers do, he wished most earnestly that it might slip on its branch and fall down before the fangs of the pack.

There was no smallest danger of the wary carcajou doing anything of the sort. Every faculty was on the alert to avenge herself on the wolves who had robbed her of her destined prey. Most of the other creatures of the wild she despised, but the wolves she also hated, because she felt herself constrained to yield them way. She crawled carefully from tree to tree, till at last she gained one whose lower branches spread directly over the carcass of the moose. Creeping out upon one of those branches, she glared down maliciously upon her foes. Observing her, two of the wolves desisted long enough from their feasting to leap up at her with fiercely gnashing teeth. But finding her out of reach, and scornfully unmoved by their futile demonstrations, they gave it up and fell again to their ravenous feasting.

The wolverene is a big cousin to the weasel, and also to the skunk. The ferocity of the weasel it shares, and the weasel's dauntless courage. Its kinship to the skunk is attested by the possession of a gland which secretes an oil of peculiarly potent malodour. The smell of this oil is not so overpowering, so pungently strangulating, as that emitted by the skunk; but all the wild creatures find it irresistibly disgusting. No matter how pinched and racked by famine they may be, not one of them will touch a morsel of meat which a wolverene has defiled ever so slightly. The wolverene itself, however, by no means shares this general prejudice.

When the carcajou had glared down upon the wolves for several minutes, she ejected the contents of her oil-gland all over the body of the moose, impartially treating her foes to a portion of the nauseating fluid. With coughing, and sneezing, and furious yelping, the wolves bounded away, and began rolling and burrowing in the snow. They could not rid themselves at once of the dreadful odour; but, presently recovering their self-possession, and resolutely ignoring the polluted meat, they ranged themselves in a circle around the tree at a safe distance, and snapped their long jaws vengefully at their adversary. They seemed prepared to stay there indefinitely, in the hope of starving out the carcajou and tearing her to pieces. Perceiving this, the carcajou turned her back upon them, climbed farther up the tree to a comfortable crotch, and settled herself indifferently for a nap. For all her voracious appetite, she knew she could go hungry longer than any wolf, and quite wear out the pack in a waiting game. Then the trapper, indignant at seeing so much good meat spoiled, but his sporting instincts stirred to sympathy by the triumph of one beast like the carcajou over a whole wolf-pack, turned his back upon the scene and resumed his tramp. The wolves had lost prestige in his eyes, and he now felt ready to fight them all with his single axe.

III

From that day on the wolf-pack cherished a sleepless grudge against the carcajou, and wasted precious hours, from time to time, striving to catch her off her guard. The wolf's memory is a long one, and the feud lost nothing in its bitterness as the winter weeks, loud with storm or still with deadly cold, dragged by. For a time the crafty old carcajou fed fat on the flesh which none but she could touch, while all the other beasts but the bear, safe asleep in his den, and the porcupine, browsing contentedly on hemlock and spruce, went lean with famine. During this period, since she had all that even her great appetite could dispose of, the carcajou robbed neither the hunter's traps nor the scant stores of the other animals. But at last her larder was bare. Then, turning her attention to the traps again, she speedily drew upon her the trapper's wrath, and found herself obliged to keep watch against two foes at once, and they the most powerful in the wilderness--namely, the man and the wolf-pack. Even the magnitude of this feud, however, did not daunt her greedy but fearless spirit, and she continued to rob the traps, elude the wolves, and evade the hunter's craftiest efforts, till the approach of spring not only eased the famine of the forest but put an end to the man's trapping. When the furs of the wild kindred began to lose their gloss and vitality, the trapper loaded his pelts upon a big hand-sledge, sealed up his cabin securely, and set out for the settlements before the snow should all be gone. Once assured of his absence, the carcajou devoted all her strength and cunning to making her way into the closed cabin. At last, after infinite patience and endeavour, she managed to get in, through the roof. There were supplies--flour, and bacon, and dried apples, all very much to her distinctly catholic taste--and she enjoyed herself immensely till private duties summoned her reluctantly away.

Spring comes late to the great snows, but when it does come it is swift and not to be denied. Then summer, with much to do and little time to do it in, rushes ardently down upon the plains and the fir-forests. About three miles back from the cabin, on a dry knoll in the heart of a tangled swamp, the old wolverene dug herself a commodious and secret burrow. Here she gave birth to a litter of tiny young ones, much like herself in miniature, only of a paler colour and softer, silkier fur. In her ardent, unflagging devotion to these little ones she undertook no hunting that would take her far from home, but satisfied her appetite with mice, slugs, worms and beetles.

Living in such seclusion as she did, her enemies the wolves lost all track of her for the time. The pack had broken up, as a formal organization, according to the custom of wolf-packs in summer. But there was still more or less cohesion, of a sort, between its scattered members; and the leader and his mate had a cave not many miles from the wolverene's retreat.

As luck would have it, the gray old leader, returning to the cave one day with the body of a rabbit between his gaunt jaws, took a short cut across the swamp, and came upon the trail of his long-lost enemy. In fact, he came upon several of her trails; and he understood very well what it meant. He had no time, or inclination, to stop and look into the matter then; but his sagacious eyes gleamed with vengeful intention as he continued his journey.

About this time--the time being a little past midsummer--the man came back to his cabin, bringing supplies. It was a long journey between the cabin and the settlements, and he had to make it several times during the brief summer, in order to accumulate stores enough to last through the long, merciless season of the great snows. When he reached the cabin and found that, in spite of all his precautions, the greedy carcajou had outwitted him and broken in, and pillaged his stores, his indignation knew no bounds.

The carcajou had become an enemy more dangerous to him than all the other beasts of the wild together. She must be hunted down and destroyed before he could go on with his business of laying in stores for the winter.

For several days the man prowled in ever-widening circles around his cabin, seeking to pick up his enemy's fresh trail. At last, late one afternoon, he found it, on the outskirts of the swamp. It was too late to follow it up then. But the next day he set out betimes with rifle, axe and spade, vowed to the extermination of the whole carcajou family, for he knew, as well as the old wolf did, why the carcajou had taken up her quarters in the swamp.

It chanced that this very morning was the morning when the wolves had undertaken to settle their ancient grudge. The old leader--his mate being occupied with her cubs--had managed to get hold of two other members of the pack, with memories as long as his. The unravelling of the trails in the swamp was an easy task for their keen noses. They found the burrow on the dry, warm knoll, prowled stealthily all about it for a few minutes, then set themselves to digging it open. When the man, whose wary, moccasined feet went noiselessly as a fox's, came in eyeshot of the knoll, the sight he caught through the dark jumble of tree-trunks brought him to a stop. He slunk behind a screen of branches and peered forth with eager interest. What he saw was three big, gray wolves, starting to dig furiously. He knew they were digging at the carcajou's burrow.

When the wolves fell to digging their noses told them that there were young carcajous in the burrow, but they could not be sure whether the old one was at home or not. On this point, however, they were presently informed. As the dry earth flew from beneath their furious claws, a dark, blunt snout shot forth, to be as swiftly withdrawn. Its appearance was followed by a yelp of pain, and one of the younger wolves drew back, walking on three legs. One fore paw had been bitten clean through, and he lay down whining, to lick and cherish it. That paw, at least, would do no more digging for some time.

The man, in his hiding-place behind the screen, saw what had happened, and felt a twinge of sympathetic admiration for his enemy, the savage little fighter in the burrow. The remaining two wolves now grew more cautious, keeping back from the entrance as well as they could, and undermining its edges. Again and again the dark muzzle shot forth, but the wolves always sprang away in time to escape punishment. This went on till the wolves had made such an excavation that the man thought they must be nearing the bottom of the den. He waited breathlessly for the denouement, which he knew would be exciting.

He had not long to wait.

On a sudden, as if jerked from a catapult, the old carcajou sprang clear out, snatching at the muzzle of the nearest wolf. He dodged, but not quite far enough; and she caught him fairly in the side of the throat, just behind the jaw. It was a deadly grip, and the wolf rose on his hind legs, struggling frantically to shake her off. But with her great strength and powerful, clutching claws, which she used almost as a bear might, she pulled him down on top of her, striving to use his bulk as a shield against the fangs of the other wolf; and the two rolled over and over to the foot of the knoll.

It was the second young wolf, unfortunately for her, that she had fastened upon, or the victory, even against such odds, might have been hers. But the old leader was wary. He saw that his comrade was done for; so he stood watchful, biding his chance to get just the grip he wanted. At length, as he saw the younger wolf's struggles growing feebler, he darted in and slashed the carcajou frightfully across the loins. But this was not the hold that he wanted. As she dropped her victim and turned upon him valiantly, he caught her high up on the back, and held her fast between his bone-crushing jaws. It was a final and fatal grip; but she was not beaten until she was dead. With her fierce eyes already glazing she writhed about and succeeded in fixing her death-grip upon the victor's lean fore leg. With the last ounce of her strength, the last impulses of her courage and her hate, she clinched her jaws till her teeth met through flesh, sinew and the cracking bone itself. Then her lifeless body went limp, and with a swing of his massive neck the old wolf flung her from him.

Having satisfied himself that she was quite dead, the old wolf now slunk off on three legs into the swamp, holding his maimed and bleeding limb as high as he could. Then the man stepped out from his hiding-place and came forward. The wolf who had been first bitten got up and limped away with surprising agility; but the one in whose throat the old carcajou had fixed her teeth lay motionless where he had fallen, a couple of paces from his dead slayer. Wolf-pelts were no good at this season, so the man thrust the body carelessly aside with his foot. But he stood for a minute or two looking down with whimsical respect on the dead form of the carcajou.

"Y' ain't nawthin' but a thief an' stinkin' Glutton," he muttered presently, "an' the whole kit an' bilin' of ye's got to be wiped out! But, when it comes to grit, clean through, I takes off my cap to ye!"

WHEN THE TRUCE OF THE WILD IS DONE

BY day it was still high summer in the woods, with slumbrous heat at noon, and the murmur of insects under the thick foliage. But to the initiated sense there was a difference. A tang in the forest scents told the nostrils that autumn had arrived. A crispness in the feel of the air, elusive but persistent, hinted of approaching frost. The still warmth was haunted, every now and then, by a passing ghost of chill. Here and there the pale green of the birches was thinly webbed with gold. Here and there a maple hung out amid its rich verdure a branch prematurely turned, glowing like a banner of aerial rose. Along the edges of the little wild meadows which bordered the loitering brooks the first thin blooms of the asters began to show, like a veil of blown smoke. In open patches, on the hillsides the goldenrod burned orange and the fireweed spread its washes of violet pink. Somewhere in the top of a tall poplar, crowning the summit of a glaring white bluff, a locust twanged incessantly its strident string. Mysteriously, imperceptibly, without sound and without warning, the change had come.

Hardly longer ago than yesterday, the wild creatures had been unwary and confident, showing themselves everywhere. The partridge coveys had whirred up noisily in full view of the passing woodsman, and craned their necks to watch him from the near-by branches. On every shallow mere and tranquil river-reach the flocks of wild ducks had fed boldly, suffering canoe or punt to come within easy gunshot. In the heavy grass of the wild meadows, or among the long, washing sedges of the lakeside, the red deer had pastured openly in the broad daylight, with tramplings and splashings, and had lifted large bright eyes of unterrified curiosity if a boat or canoe happened by. The security of that great truce, which men called "close season" had rested sweetly on the forest.

Then suddenly, when the sunrise was pink on the mists, a gunshot had sent the echoes clamouring across the still lake waters, and a flock of ducks, flapping up and fleeing with frightened cries, had left one of its members sprawling motionless among the flattened sedge, a heap of bright feathers spattered with blood. Later in the morning a rifle had cracked sharply on the hillside, and a little puff of white smoke had blown across the dark front of the fir groves. The truce had come to an end.

All summer long men had kept the truce with strictness, and the hunter's fierce instinct, curbed alike by law and foresight, had slumbered. But now the young coveys were full-fledged and strong of wing, well able to care for themselves. The young ducks were full grown, and no longer needed their mother's guardianship and teaching. The young deer were learning to shift for themselves, and finding, to their wonder and indignation, that their mothers grew day by day more indifferent to them, more inclined to wander off in search of new interests. The time had come when the young of the wilderness stood no longer in need of protection. Then the hand of the law was lifted.

Instantly in the hearts of men the hunter's fever flamed up, and, with eager eyes, they went forth to kill. Where they had yesterday walked openly, hardly heeding the wild creatures about them, they now crept stealthily, following the trails, or lying in ambush, waiting for the unsuspicious flock to wing past. And when they found that the game, yesterday so abundant and unwatchful, had to-day almost wholly disappeared, they were indignant, and wished that they had anticipated the season by a few hours.

As a matter of fact, the time of the ending of the truce was not the same for all the wild creatures which had profited by its protection through the spring and summer. Certain of the tribes, according to the law's provisions, were secure for some weeks longer yet. But this they never seemed to realize. As far as they could observe, when the truce was broken for one it was broken for all, and all took alarm together. In some unexplained way, perhaps by the mere transmission of a general fear, word went around that the time had come for invisibility and craft. All at once, therefore, as it seemed to men, the wilderness had become empty.

Down a green, rough wood-road, leading from the Settlement to one of the wild meadows by the river, came a young man in homespun carrying a long, old-fashioned, muzzle-loading duck-gun. Two days before this he had seen a fine buck, with antlers perfect and new-shining from the velvet, feeding on the edge of this meadow. The young woodsman had his gun loaded with buckshot. He wanted both venison and a pair of horns; and, knowing the fancy of the deer for certain favourite pastures, he had great hopes of finding the buck somewhere about the place where he had last seen him. With flexible "larrigans" of oiled cowhide on his feet, the hunter moved noiselessly and swiftly as a panther, his keen pale-blue eyes peering from side to side through the shadowy undergrowth. Not three steps aside from the path, moveless as a stone and invisible among the spotted weeds and twigs, a crafty old cock-partridge stood with head erect and unwinking eyes and watched the dangerous intruder stride by.

Approaching the edge of the open, the young hunter kept himself carefully hidden behind the fringing leafage and looked forth upon the little meadow. No creature being in sight, he cut straight across the grass to the water's edge, and scanned the muddy margin for foot-prints. These he presently found in abundance, along between grass and sedge. Most of the marks were old; but others were so fresh that he knew the buck must have been there and departed within the last ten minutes. Into some deep hoof-prints the water was still oozing, while from others the trodden stems of sedge were slowly struggling upright.

A smile of keen satisfaction passed over the young woodsman's face at these signs. He prided himself on his skill in trailing, and the primeval predatory elation thrilled his nerves. At a swift but easy lope he took up that clear trail, and followed it back through the grass toward the woods. It entered the woods not ten paces from the point where the hunter himself had emerged, ran parallel with the old wood-road for a dozen yards, and came to a plain halt in the heart of a dense thicket of hemlock. From the thicket it went off in great leaps in a direction at right angles to the path. There was not a breath of wind stirring, to carry a scent. So the hunter realized that his intended victim had been watching him from the thicket, and that it was now a case of craft against craft. He tightened his belt for a long chase, and set his lean jaws doggedly as he resumed the trail.

The buck, who was wise with the wisdom of experience, and apprised by the echoes of the first gunshot of the fact that the truce was over, had indeed been watching the hunter very sagaciously. The moment he was satisfied that it was his trail the hunter was following, he had set out at top speed, anxious to get as far as possible from so dangerous a neighbourhood. At first his fear grew with his flight, so that his great, soft eyes stared wildly and his nostrils dilated as he went bounding over all obstacles. Then little by little the triumphant exercise of his powers, and a realization of how far his speed surpassed that of his pursuer, reassured him somewhat. He decided to rest, and find out what his foe was doing. He doubled back parallel with his own trail for about fifty yards, then lay down in a thicket to watch the enemy go by.

In an incredibly short time he did go by, at that long, steady swing which ate up the distance so amazingly. As soon as he was well past, the buck sprang up and was off again at full speed, his heart once more thumping with terror.

This time, however, instead of running straight ahead, he made a wide, sweeping curve, tending back toward the river and the lakes. As before, only somewhat sooner, his alarm subsided and his confidence, along with his curiosity, returned. He repeated his former manoeuvre of doubling back a little way upon his trail, then again lay down to wait for the passing of his foe.

When the hunter came to that first abrupt turn of the trail he realized that it was a cunning and experienced buck with which he had to deal. He smiled confidently, however, feeling sure of his own skill, and ran at full speed to the point where the animal had lain down to watch him pass. From this point he followed the trail just far enough to catch its curve. Then he left it and ran in a straight line shrewdly calculated to form the chord to his quarry's section of a circle. His plan was to intercept and pick up the trail again about three quarters of a mile further on. In nine cases out of ten his calculation would have worked out as he wished; but in this case he had not made allowance for this particular buck's individuality. While he imagined his quarry to be yet far ahead, he ran past a leafy clump of mingled Indian pear and thick spruce seedlings. Half a minute later he heard a crash of underbrush behind him. As he turned he caught a tantalizing glimpse of tawny haunches vanishing through the green, and he knew that once again he had been outplayed.

This time the wise buck was distinctly more terrified than before. The appearance of his enemy at this unexpected point, so speedily, and not upon the trail, struck a panic to his heart. Plainly, this was no common foe, to be evaded by familiar stratagems. His curiosity and his confidence disappeared completely.

The buck set off in a straight line for the river, now perhaps a half-mile distant. Reaching it, he turned down the shore, running in the shallow water to cover his scent. It never occurred to him that his enemy was trailing him by sight, not by scent; so he followed the same tactics he would have employed had the pursuer been a wolf or a dog. A hundred yards further on he rounded a sharp bend of the stream. Here he took to deep water, swam swiftly to the opposite shore, and vanished into the thick woods.

Two or three minutes later the man came out upon the river's edge. The direction his quarry had taken was plainly visible by the splashes of water on the rocks, and he smiled grimly at the precaution which the animal had taken to cover his secret. But when he reached the point where the buck had taken to deep water the smile faded. He stopped, leaning on his gun and staring across the river, and a baffled look came over his face. Realizing, after a few moments, that he was beaten in this game, he drew out his charge of buckshot, reloaded his gun with small duckshot, and hid himself in a waterside covert of young willows, in the hope that a flock of mallard or teal might presently come by.

THE WINDOW IN THE SHACK

THE attitude in which the plump baby hung limply over the woman's left arm looked most uncomfortable. The baby, however, seemed highly content. Both his sticky fists clutched firmly a generous "chunk" of new maple-sugar, which he mumbled with his toothless gums, while his big eyes, widening like an owl's, stared about through the dusk with a placid intentness.

From the woman's left hand dangled an old tin lantern containing a scrap of tallow candle, whose meagre gleam flickered hither and thither apprehensively among the huge shadows of the darkening wood. In her right hand the woman carried a large tin bucket, half filled with fresh-run maple-sap. By the glimmer of the ineffectual candle, she moved wearily from one great maple to another, emptying the birch-bark cups that hung from the little wooden taps driven into the trunks. The night air was raw with the chill of thawing snow, and carried no sound but the soft tinkle of the sap as it dript swiftly into the birchen cups. The faint, sweet smell of the sap seemed to cling upon the darkness. The candle flared up for an instant, revealing black, mysterious aisles among the ponderous tree-trunks, then guttered down and almost went out, the darkness seeming to swoop in upon its defeat. The woman examined it, found that it was all but done, and glanced nervously over her shoulder. Then she made anxious haste to empty and replace the last of the birchen cups before she should be left in darkness to grope her way back to the cabin.

The sap was running freely that spring, and the promise of a great sugar-harvest was not to be ignored. Dave Stone's house and farm lay about three miles distant, across the valley of the "Tin Kittle," from the maple-clad ridge of forest wherein he had his sugar-camp. The camp consisted of a little cabin or "shack" of rough boards and an open shed with a rude but spacious fireplace and chimney to accommodate the great iron pot in which the sap was boiled down into sugar. While the sap was running freely, the pot had to be kept boiling uniformly and the thickening sap kept skimmed clean of the creaming scum; and therefore, during the season, some one had to be always living in the camp.

Dave Stone had built his camp at an opening in the woods, in such a position that, from its own little window in the rear, he could look out across the wide valley of the "Tin Kittle" to a rigid grove of firs behind which, shielded from the nor'easters, lay his low frame house, and red-doored barn, and wide, liberal sheds. The distance was only about three miles, or less, from the house to the sugar-camp. But Dave Stone was terribly proud of the prosperous little homestead which he had carved for himself out of the unbroken wilderness on the upper "Tin Kittle," and more than proud of the slim, gray-eyed wife and three sturdy youngsters to whom that homestead gave happy shelter. On the spring nights when he had to stay over at the camp, he liked to be able to see the grove that hid his home.

It chanced one afternoon, just in the height of the sap-running, that Dave Stone was called suddenly in to the settlement on a piece of business that could not wait overnight. A note which he had endorsed for a friend had been allowed to go to protest, and Dave was excited.

"Ther' ain't nothin' fer it, Mandy," said he, "but fer ye to take the baby an' go right over to the camp fer the night, an' keep an eye on this bilin'."

"But, father," protested his wife, in a doubtful voice, "how kin I leave Lidy an' Joe here alone?"

"Oh, there ain't nothin' goin' to bother them, an' Lidy 'most ten year old!" insisted Dave, who was in a hurry. "Don't fret, mother. I'll be back long afore mornin'!"

As the children had no objection to being left, Mrs. Stone suffered herself to be persuaded. In fact, she went to her new duty with a certain zest, as a break in the monotony of her days. She had lent a hand often enough at the sugar-making to be familiar with the task awaiting her, and it was with an unwonted gaiety that she set out on what appeared to her almost in the light of a little adventure.

But it was later than she had intended when she actually got away, the baby crowing joyously on her arm, and the children calling gay good-byes to her from the open door. Jake, the big brown retriever, tried to follow her; and when she ordered him back to stay with the children, he obeyed with a whimpering reluctance that came near rebellion. As she descended the valley, her feet sinking in the snow of the thawing trail, she wondered why the dog, which had always preferred the children, should have grown so anxious to be with her.

When she reached the camp, she was already tired, but the pleasant excitement was still upon her. When she had skimmed the big, slow-bubbling pot of syrup, tested a ladleful of it in the snow, poured in some fresh sap, and replenished the sluggish fire, dusk was already stealing upon the forest. In her haste she did not notice that the candle in the old lantern was almost burned out. Snatching up the lantern, which it was not yet necessary to light, and the big tin sap-bucket, and giving the baby, who had begun to fret, a lump of hard sugar to keep him quiet on her arm, she hurried off to tend the farthest trees before the darkness should close down upon the silences.

* * * * *

When the last birch cup had been emptied into the bucket, the candle flickered out; and for a moment or two the sudden blackness seemed to flap in her face, daunting her. She stood perfectly still till her eyes readjusted themselves. She was dead tired, the baby and the brimming bucket were heavy, and the adventurous flavour had quite gone out of her task.

In part because of her fatigue, she grew suddenly timorous. Her ears began to listen with terrible intentness till they imagined stealthy footsteps in the silken shrinkings of the damp snow. At last her eyes mastered the gloom till she could make out the glimmering pathway, the dim, black trunks shouldering up on either side of it, the clumps of bushes obstructing it here and there. Trembling--clutching tightly at the baby, the lantern, and the sap-bucket--she started back with furtive but hurried footsteps, afraid to make any noise lest she attract the notice of some mysterious powers of the wilderness.

As the woman went, her fears grew with her haste till only the difficulties of the path, with the weight of her burdens, prevented her from breaking into a run of panic. The baby, meanwhile, kept on sucking his maple-sugar and staring into the novel darkness. The woman's breath began to come too fast, her knees began to feel as if they might turn to water at any moment. At last, when within perhaps fifty paces of the shack, to her infinite relief she saw a dark, tall figure take shape just over the top of a bush, at the turn of the trail. She had room for but one thought. It was Dave, back earlier than he had expected. She did not stop to wonder how or why. With a little, breathless cry, she exclaimed: "Oh, Dave, I'm so glad! Take the baby!" and reached forward to place the little one in his arms.

Even as she did so, however, something in the tall, dim shape rising over the bush struck her as unfamiliar. And why didn't Dave speak? She paused, she half drew back, while a chill fear made her cheeks prickle; and as she slightly changed her position, the dark form grew more definite. She saw the massive bulk of the shoulders. She caught a glint of white teeth, of fierce, wild eyes.

With a screech of intolerable horror, she shrank back, clutching the baby to her bosom, swung the brimming bucket of sap full into the monster's face, and fled with the speed of a deer down another trail toward the shack. She was at the door before her appalled brain realized that the being to which she had tried to hand over the child was a huge bear.

Bewildered and abashed for a few seconds by the deluge of liquid and the clatter of the tin vessel in his face, the animal had not instantly pursued. But he was just out of the den after his long winter sleep and savage with hunger. Moreover, he had been allowed to realize that the dreaded man-creature which he had met so unexpectedly was afraid of him! He came crashing over the bushes, and was so close at the woman's heels that she had barely time to slam the shack door in his face.

As she dropped the rude wooden latch into place, the woman realized with horror how frail the door was. Momentarily she expected to see it smashed in by a stroke of the monster's paw. She did not know a bear's caution, his cunning suspicion of traps, his dread of the scent of man.

There was no light in the shack, except a faint red gleam from the open draft of the stove, and the gray pallor of the night sky glimmering in through the little window. The woman was so faint with fear that she dared not search for the candles, but leaned panting against the wall and staring at the window as if she expected the bear to look in at her. She was brought to her senses in a moment, however, by the baby beginning to cry. In the race for the shack, he had lost his lump of sugar, and now he realized how uncomfortable he was. The woman seated herself on the bench by the stove and began to nurse him, all the time keeping her eyes on the pale square of the window.

When the door was slammed in his face, the bear had backed away in apprehension and paused to study the shack. But at the sound of the baby's voice he seemed to realize that here, at least, were some individuals of the dreaded man tribe who were not dangerous. He came forward and sniffed loudly along the crack of the door till the woman's heart stood still. He leaned against it, tentatively, till it creaked, but the latch and hinges held. Then he prowled around the shack, examining it carefully, and doubtless expecting to find an open entrance somewhere. In his experience, all caves and dens had entrances. At last the window caught his attention. The woman heard the scratching of his claws on the rough outer boarding as he raised himself. Then the window was darkened by a great black head looking in.

Throwing the baby into the bunk, the woman snatched from the stove a blazing stick, rushed to the window with it, and made a wild thrust at the dreadful face. With a crash the glass flew to splinters, and the black face disappeared. The bear was untouched, but the fiery weapon had taught him discretion. He drew back with an angry growl, and sat down on his haunches as if to see what the woman would do next. She, for her part, after this victory, grew terribly afraid of setting the dry shack on fire; so she hurriedly returned the snapping, sparkling brand to the stove. Thereupon the bear resumed his ominous prowling, round and round the shack, sometimes testing the foundations and the door with massive but stealthy paw, sometimes sniffing loudly at the cracks; and the woman returned to the comforting of the baby.

In time the little one, fed full and cherished, went to sleep. Then, with nothing left to occupy her mind but the terrors of her situation, the woman found those stealthy scratchings and sniffings, and the strain of the silences that fell between, were more than she could endure. At first, she thought of getting a couple of blazing sticks, throwing open the shack door, and deliberately attacking her besieger. But this idea she dismissed as quite too desperate and futile. Then she remembered that bears were fond of sweets. A table in the corner was heaped with great, round cakes of fragrant sugar, the shape of the pans in which they had been cooled. One of these she snatched up, and threw it out of the window. The bear promptly came around to see what had dropped, and fell upon the offering with such ardour that it vanished between his great jaws in half a minute. Then he came straight to the window for more, and the woman served it out to him without delay.

The beast's appetite for maple-sugar was amazing, and as the woman saw the sweet store swiftly disappearing, her fear began to be tempered with indignation. But when her outraged frugality led her to delay the dole, her tormentor came at the window so savagely that she made all haste to supply him, and fell to wondering helplessly what she should do when the sugar was all gone.

As she stood at the window, watching fearfully the vague, monstrous shape of the animal as he pawed and gnawed at the last cake, suddenly, far across the shadowy valley, a red light leaped into the sky. For a moment the woman stared at it with an absent mind, absorbed in her own trouble, yet noticing how black and sharp, like giant spears upthrust in array, the tops of the firs stood out against the glow. For a moment she stood so staring. Then she realized where that wild light came from. With a cry she turned, rushed to the door, and tore it open. But as the dark of the forest confronted her, she remembered! Slamming and latching the door again, she rushed madly back to the window, and stood there clutching the frame with both hands, praying, and sobbing, and raving.

And the bear, having finished the sugar, sat up on his haunches to gaze intently, ears cocked and jaws half open, at that far-off, fiery brightness in the sky of night.

As the keen tongues of flame shot over the treetops, the woman clutched at her senses, and tried to persuade herself that it was the barn, not the house, that was burning. It was, in truth, quite impossible to discern, at that distance, which it was. It was not both; of that she was certain. She also told herself that, if it was the house, it was too early for the children to be asleep; and even if they were asleep, Jake would wake them; and presently some neighbours, who were not more than a mile away, would come to comfort their fears and shelter them. She would not allow herself to harbour the awful thought that the fire might have caught the children in their sleep. Nevertheless, do what she could to fight it away, the hideous suggestion kept clamouring at her brain, driving her to a frenzy. Had she been alone in this crisis, the great beast watching and prowling outside the shack would have had no terrors for her. But the baby! She could not run fast with that burden. She could not leave him behind in the bunk, for the bear would either climb in the window or batter in the door when she was gone. Yet to stand idle and watch those leaping flames--that way lay madness. Again her mind reverted to the blazing brand with which she had driven the bear from the window. If she took one big enough and carried it with her, the bear would probably not dare even to follow her. She sprang eagerly to the stove, but the fire was already dying down. It was nothing but a heap of coals, and in her stress she had not noticed how cold it had grown in the shack. She looked for wood, but there was none. She had forgotten to bring in an armful from the pile over by the sugar-boiler. Well, the plan had been an insane one, hopeless from the first. But, at least, it had been a plan. The failure of it seemed to leave her tortured brain a blank. But the cold--that was an impression that pierced her despair. She went to the bunk, and covered the sleeping baby with warm blankets. As she leaned over him, she heard the bear again, sniffing, sniffing along the crack at the bottom of the door. She almost laughed--that the beast should want anything more after all that sugar! Then she felt herself sinking, and clutched at the edge of the bunk to save herself. She would lie down by the baby! But instead of that she sank upon the floor in a huddled heap.

Her swoon must have passed imperceptibly into the heavy sleep of emotional exhaustion, for she lay unstirring for some hours. The crying of the little one awoke her.

Stiff, half frozen, utterly dazed, she pulled herself up to the bunk, nursed the child, and soothed him again to sleep. Then the accumulation of anguish which had overwhelmed her rolled back upon her understanding. She staggered to the window.

The dreadful illumination across the valley had died down to a faint ruddiness, just seen through the thin tops of the firs. The fire--whether it had been the barn or the house--had burned itself out. Whatever had happened, it was over. As she stood shuddering, unable to think, not daring to think, her eyes rested upon the bear, huge and formless in the gloom, staring at her, not ten feet away. She answered the stare fixedly, no longer aware of fearing him. Then she saw him turn his head suddenly, as if he had heard something. And the next moment he had faded away swiftly and noiselessly into the darkness, like a startled partridge. She heard quick footsteps coming up the trail. A dog's fierce growl broke into a bark of warning. That was Jake's bark! She almost threw herself at the door, and tore it open.

* * * * *

Dave Stone had got back from the settlement earlier than he expected, driving furiously the last two miles of his journey, with his eyes full of the red light of that burning, his heart gripped with intolerable fear. He had found his good barn in flames, but the children safe, the house untouched, the stock rescued. The children, prompt and resourceful as the children of the backwoods have need to be, had loosed the cattle from the stanchions and got them out in time. Neighbours, hurrying up in response to the flaming summons, had found the children watching the blaze enthusiastically from the doorstep, as if it had been arranged for their amusement. Seeing matters so much better than they might have been, Dave was struck with a new apprehension, because Mandy had not returned. It was hardly conceivable that she had failed to see the flames from the window of the shack! Then why had she not come? Followed by Jake, he had taken the camp trail at a run to find out what was the matter.

As he drew near the shack, the darkness of it chilled him with dread. No firelight gleam showed out from the window! And no red glow came from the boiling-shed! The fire had been allowed to die out under the sugar-pot! As the significance of this dawned upon him, his keen woodsman's eyes seemed to detect through the dark a shape of thicker blackness gliding past the shack and into the woods. At the same moment Jake growled, barked shortly, and dashed past him, with the hair bristling along his neck.

The man's blood went to ice, as he sprang to the door of the shack, crying in a terrible voice: "Mandy! Mandy! Where are--" But before the question was out of his mouth, the door leaped open, and Mandy was on his neck, shaking and sobbing.

"The children?" she gasped.

"Why, they're all right, mother!" replied the man cheerfully. "It was only the barn--an' they got the critters out all safe! But what's wrong here? An' what's kep' you? An' didn't you--"

But he was not allowed to finish his questionings, for the woman was crying and laughing and strangling him with her wild clasp. "Oh, Dave!" she managed to exclaim. "It was the bear--as tried to git us--all night long! An' he's et up every crum of the last bilin'."

THE RETURN OF THE MOOSE

"TO the best of my knowledge, ther' ain't been no moose seen this side the river these eighteen year back."

The speaker, a heavy-shouldered, long-legged backwoodsman, paused in his task of digging potatoes, leaned on the handle of his broad-tined digging fork, and bit off a liberal chew from his plug of black tobacco. His companion, digging parallel with him on the next row, paused sympathetically, felt in his trousers' pocket for his own plug of "black jack," and cast a contemplative eye up the wide brown slope of the potato-field toward the ragged and desolate line of burnt woods which crested the hill.

The woods, a long array of erect, black, fire-scarred rampikes, appeared to scrawl the very significance of solitude against the lonely afternoon sky. The austerity of the scene was merely heightened by the yellow glow of a birch thicket at the further upper corner of the potato-field, and by the faint tints of violet light that flowed over the brown soil from a pallid and fading sunset. As the sky was scrawled by the gray-and-black rampikes, so the slope was scrawled by zigzag lines of gray-and-black snake fence, leading down to three log cabins, with their cluster of log barns and sheds, scattered irregularly along a terrace of the slope. A quarter of a mile further down, beyond the little gray dwellings, a sluggish river wound between alder swamps and rough wild meadows.

As the second potato-digger was lifting his plug of tobacco to his mouth, his hand stopped half way, and his grizzled jaw dropped in astonishment. For a couple of seconds he stared at the ragged hill-crest. Then, it being contrary to his code to show surprise, he bit off his chew, returned the tobacco to his pocket, and coolly remarked: "Well, I reckon they've come back."

"What do you mean?" demanded the first speaker, who had resumed his digging.

"There be your moose, after these eighteen year!" said the other.

Standing out clear of the dead forest, and staring curiously down upon the two potato-diggers, were three moose,--a magnificent, black, wide-antlered bull, an ungainly brown cow, and a long-legged, long-eared calf. A potato-field, with men digging in it, was something far apart from their experience and manifestly filled them with interest.

"Keep still now, Sandy," muttered the first speaker, who was wise in the ways of the wood-folk. "Keep still till they git used to us. Then we'll go for our guns."

The men stood motionless for a couple of minutes, and the moose came further into the open in order to get a better look at them. Then, leaving their potato forks standing in their furrows, the men strode quietly down the field, down the rocky pasture lane, and into the nearest house. Here the man called Sandy got down his gun,--an old muzzle-loading, single-barrelled musket,--and hurriedly loaded it with buckshot; while the other, who was somewhat the more experienced hunter, ran on to the next cabin and got his big Snider rifle. The moose, meanwhile, having watched the men fairly indoors, turned aside and fell to browsing on the tiny poplar saplings which grew along the top of the field.

Saying nothing to their people in the houses, after the reticent backwoods fashion, Sandy and Lije strolled carelessly down the road till the potato-field was hidden from sight by a stretch of young second-growth spruce and fir. Up through this cover they ran eagerly, bending low, and gained the forest of rampikes on top of the hill. Here they circled widely, crouching in the coarse weeds and dodging from trunk to trunk, until they knew they were directly behind the potato-field. Then they crept noiselessly outward toward the spot where they had last seen the moose. The wind was blowing softly into their faces, covering their scent; and their dull gray homespun clothes fitted the colour of the desolation around them.

Now it chanced that the big bull had changed his mind, and wandered back among the rampikes, leaving the cow and calf at their browsing among the poplars. The woodsmen, therefore, came upon him unexpectedly. Not thirty yards distant, he stood eying them with disdainful curiosity, his splendid antlers laid back while he thrust forward his big, sensitive nose, trying to get the wind of these mysterious strangers. There was menace in his small, watchful eyes, and altogether his appearance was so formidable that the hunters were just a trifle flurried, and fired too hastily. The big bullet of Lije's Snider went wide, while a couple of Sandy's buckshot did no more than furrow the great beast's shoulder. The sudden pain and the sudden monstrous noise filled him with rage, and, with an ugly grunting roar, he charged.

"Up a tree, Sandy!" yelled Lije, setting the example. But the bull was so close at his heels that he could not carry his rifle with him. He dropped it at the foot of the tree, and swung himself up into the dead branches just in time to escape the animal's rearing plunge.

Sandy, meanwhile, had found himself in serious plight, there being no suitable refuge just at hand. Those trees which were big enough had had no branches spared by the fire. He had to run some distance. Just as he was hesitating as to what he should do, and looking for a rock or stump behind which he might hide while he reloaded his gun, the moose caught sight of him, forgot about Lije, and came charging through the weeds. Sandy had no more time for hesitation. He dropped his unwieldy musket, and clambered into a blackened and branchy hackmatack, so small that he feared the rush of the bull might break it down. It did, indeed, crack ominously when the headlong bulk reared upon it; but it stood. And Sandy felt as if every branch he grasped were an eggshell.

Seeing that the bull's attention was so well occupied, Lije slipped down the further side of his tree and recaptured his Snider. He had by this time entirely recovered his nerve, and now felt master of the situation. Having slipped in a new cartridge he stood forth boldly and waited for the moose to offer him a fair target. As the animal moved this way and that, he at length presented his flank. The big Snider roared; and he dropped with a ball through his heart, dead instantly. Sandy came down from his little tree, and touched the huge dark form and mighty antlers with admiring awe.

In the meantime, the noise of the firing had thrown the cow and calf into a panic. Since the woods behind them were suddenly filled with such thunders, they could not flee in that direction. But far below them, down the brown slopes and past the gray cabins, they saw the river gleaming among its alder thickets. There was the shelter they craved; and down the fields they ran, with long, shambling, awkward strides that took them over the ground at a tremendous pace. At the foot of the field they blundered into the lane leading down to Sandy's cabin.

Now, as luck would have it, Sandy had that summer decided to build himself a frame house to supplant the old log cabin. As a preliminary, he had dug a spacious cellar, just at the foot of the lane. It was deep as well as wide, being intended for the storage of many potatoes. And, in order to prevent any of the cattle from falling into it, he had surrounded it with a low fence which chanced to be screened along the upper side with a rank growth of burdock and other barnyard weeds.

When the moose cow reached this fence, she hardly noticed it. She was used to striding over obstacles. Just now her heart was mad with panic, and her eyes full of the gleam of the river she was seeking. She cleared the fence without an effort--and went crashing to the bottom of the cellar. Not three paces behind her came the calf.

By this time, of course, all the little settlement was out, and the flight of the cow and calf down the field had been followed with eager eyes. Everyone ran at once to the cellar. The unfortunate cow was seen to have injured herself so terribly by the plunge that, without waiting for the owner of the cellar to return, the young farmer from the third cabin jumped down and ended her suffering with a butcher knife. The calf, however, was unhurt. He stood staring stupidly at his dead mother and showed no fear of the people that came up to stroke and admire him. He seemed so absolutely docile that when Sandy and Lije came proudly down the hill to tell of their achievement, Sandy declared that the youngster should be kept and made a pet of.

"Seems to me," he said to Lije, "that seein' as the moose had been so long away, we hain't treated them jest right when they come back. I feel like we'd ought to make it up to the little feller."

FROM THE TEETH OF THE TIDE

HITHERTO, ever since he had been old enough to leave the den, the mother bear had been leading her fat black cub inland, among the tumbled rocks and tangled spruce and pine, teaching him to dig for tender roots and nose out grubs and beetles from the rotting stumps. To-day, feeling the need of saltier fare, she led him in the opposite direction, down through a cleft in the cliffs, and out across the great, red, glistening mud-flats left bare by the ebb of the terrific Fundy tides.

From the secure warmth of his den the cub had heard, faint and far off, the waves thundering along the bases of the cliffs, when the tide was high and the great winds drew heavily in from sea. The sound had always made him afraid; and to-day, though there was no wind, and the tide was so far out that it made no noise but a soft whisper, silken and persuasive, he held back with babyish timidity, till his mother brought him to his senses with an unceremonious cuff on the side of the head. With a squall of grieved surprise he picked himself up, shaking his head as if he had a bee in his ear, and then made haste to follow obediently, close at his mother's huge black heels.

From the break in the cliffs, where the bears came down, ran a ledge of shelving rocks on a long, gradual slant across the flats toward the edge of low water. The tide was nearing the last of the ebb; and now, the slope of the shore being very gradual, and the difference between high and low water in these turbulent channels something between forty and fifty feet, the lapsing fringes of the ebb, yellow-tawny with silt, were a good three-quarters of a mile away from the foot of the cliffs. The vast spaces between were smooth, oily, copper-red mud, shining and treacherous in the sun with the narrow black outcrop of the ledge drawn across on so gentle a slant that before it reached the water it was running almost on a parallel with the shoreline.

Along the rocky ledge the old bear led the way, pausing to nose at a patch of seaweed here and there or to glance shrewdly into the shallow pools among the rocks. The cub obediently followed her example, though doubtless with no idea of what he might hope to find. But the upper stretches of the ledge, near high-water mark, offered nothing to reward their quest, having been dry for several hours, and long ago thoroughly gone over by earlier foragers. So the bears pushed on down toward the lower stretches, where the ledges were still wet, and the long, black-green weed-masses still dripping, and where the limpet-covered protuberances of rock still oozed and sparkled. With her iron-hard claws the mother bear scraped off a quantity of these limpets, and crushed them between her jaws with relish, swallowing the salty juices. The cub tried clumsily to imitate her, but the limpets defied his too tender claws, so he ran to his mother, thrust her great head aside, and greedily licked up a share of her scrapings. The sea flavour tickled his palate, but the rough, hard shells exasperated him. They hurt his gums, so that he merely rolled them over in his mouth, sucked at them a few moments, then spat them out indignantly. His mother thereupon forsook the unsatisfactory limpets, and went prowling on toward the water's edge in search of more satisfying fare. As they left the limpets, a gaunt figure in gray homespuns, carrying a rifle, appeared on the crest of the cliffs above, caught sight of them, and hurriedly took cover behind an overhanging pine.

The young woodsman's first impulse was to try a long shot at the hulking black shape so conspicuous out on the ledge, against the bright water. He wanted a bearskin, even if the fur was not just then in prime condition. But more particularly he wanted the cub, to tame and play with if it should prove amenable, and to sell, ultimately, for a good amount, to some travelling show. On consideration, he decided to lie in wait among the rocks till the rising tide should drive the bears back to the upland. He exchanged his steel-nosed cartridges for the more deadly mushroom-tipped, filled his pipe, and lay back comfortably against the pine trunk, to watch, through the thin green frondage, the foraging of his intended prey.

The farther they went down the long slant of the ledge, the more interested the bears became. Here the crows and gulls had not had time to capture all the prizes. There were savoury blue-shelled mussels clinging under the tips of the rocks; plump, spiral whelks between the oozy tresses of the seaweed;

orange starfish and bristly sea-urchins in the shallow pools. All these dainties had shells that the cub's young teeth could easily crush, and they yielded meaty morsels that made beetles and grubs seem very meagre fare. Moreover, in the salty bitter of this sea-fruit there was something marvelously stimulating to the appetite. From pool to pool the old bear wandered on, lured ever by richer prizes just ahead; and the cub, stuffed till his little stomach was like a black furry ball, no longer frisked and tumbled, but waddled along beside her with eyes of shining expectancy. As long as he was not too full to walk, he was not too full to eat such delicacies as these. The fascinating quest led them on and on till at last they found themselves at the water's edge.

By this time they had travelled a long way from the cleft in the cliffs by which they had come down from the uplands. A good half-mile of shining mud separated them, in a direct line, from the cliff base. And the woodsman on the height, as he watched them, muttered to himself: "Ef that old b'ar don't look out, the tide's a-goin' to ketch her afore she knows what she's about! Most wish I'd 'a' socked it to her afore she'd got so fur out--Jiminy! She's seed her mistake now! The tide's turned."

While bear and cub had their noses and paws busy in a little dry pool, on a sudden a long, shallow, muddy-crested wave had come hissing up over their feet and filled the pool to the brim with its yellow flood. Lifting her head sharply, the old bear glanced at the far-off cliffs, and at the mounting tide. Instantly realizing the peril, she started back at a slow, lumbering amble up the long, long path by which they had come; and the cub started too at a brave gallop--not behind her, for he was too much afraid of the hissing yellow wave, but close at her side, between her sheltering form and the shore. He felt that she could in some way ward off or subdue the cold and terrifying monster.

For perhaps two minutes the cub struggled on gamely, although, owing to the fact that at this point their path was almost parallel with the water, the fugitives made no perceptible gain, and the rising wave was on their heels every instant. Then the greedy feeding produced its effect. The little fellow's wind gave out completely. With a whimper of pain and fright he dropped back upon his haunches and waited for his mother to save him.

The old bear turned, bounced back, and cuffed him so bruskly that he found breath enough to utter a loud squall and go stumbling forward for another score of yards. Then he gave out, and sank upon his too-distended stomach, whimpering piteously.

This time the mother seemed to perceive that his case was serious, and her anxious wrath subsided. She licked him assiduously for a few seconds, whining encouragement, till at last he got upon his feet again, trembling. The yellow flood was now lapping on the ledge all about them. But a rod or two farther on the rocks bulged up a couple of feet above the surrounding slope. Thrusting the exhausted youngster ahead of her with nose and paws, the old bear gained this point of temporary vantage; and then, worried and frightened, sat down upon her haunches and stared all around her, as if trying to decide what should be done. The cub lay flat, with legs outstretched and mouth wide open, panting.

The tide, meanwhile, was mounting so swiftly that in a few moments the rise of rocks had become almost an island. The ledge was covered before them as well as behind, and the only way still open lay straight over the glistening mud. The old bear looked at it, and whined, knowing its treacheries. And the woodsman, watching with eager interest from the cliffs, muttered:

"Take to it, ye old bug-eater! Ther' ain't nawthin' else left fer ye to do'!"

This was apparently the conclusion of the old bear herself; for now, after licking and nuzzling the cub for a few seconds till he stood up, she stepped boldly off the rock and started out over the coppery flats. The cub, having apparently recovered his wind, followed briskly--probably much heartened by the fact that his progress was in a direction away from the alarming waves.

There was desperate need of haste, for when they left the rocky lift the tide was already slipping around upon the flats beyond it. Nevertheless, the old bear moved with deliberation. She could not hurry the cub; and she had to choose her path. By some instinct, or else by some peculiar keenness of observation, she seemed to detect the "honey-pots," or deep pockets of slime, that lay concealed beneath the uniformly shining surface of the mud; for here she would make an aimless detour, losing many precious seconds, and there she would side-step suddenly, for several paces, and shift her course to a new parallel. Outside the "honey-pots," the mud was soft and tenacious to a depth varying from a few inches to a couple of feet, but with a hard clay foundation beneath the slime. Through this clinging red ooze the old bear, with her huge strength, made her way without difficulty; but the cub, in a few moments, began to find himself terribly hampered. His fur collected the mud. His little paws sank easily, but at each step it grew harder to withdraw them. At last, chancing to stagger aside from his mother's spacious tracks, he sank to his belly in the rim of a "honey-pot."

Panic-stricken, he floundered vainly, his nose high in the air and his eyes shut tight, while his mother, unconscious of what had happened, ploughed doggedly onward. Presently he opened his eyes. His mother was now perhaps ten or a dozen feet ahead, apparently deserting him. Right behind, lapping up to his very tail, was the crawling wave. A heart-broken bawl burst from his throat.

At that cry the old bear came dashing back, red mud half-way up her flanks and plastered all over her shaggy chest. Taking in the situation at a glance, she seized the cub by the nape of the neck with her teeth, and tried to drag him free. But he squealed so lamentably that she realized that the hide would yield before the mud would. The attempt had taken time, however; and the tide was now well up in the fur of his back. Thrusting her paw down beneath his haunches, she tore him clear with a mighty wrench and a loud sucking of the baffled mud. That stroke sent him head over heels some ten feet nearer safety. By the time he had picked himself up, pawing fretfully at the mud that bedaubed his face and half blinded him, his mother was close behind him, nosing him along and lifting him forward skilfully with her fore paws.

The slope of the flats was now so gradual as to be almost imperceptible; and the tide, therefore, seemed to be racing in with fiercer haste, as if in wrath at being so long balked of its prey. Engrossed in her efforts to push the cub forward, the mother now lost some of her fine discrimination in regard to "honey-pots." She pushed the cub straight into one; but jerked him back unceremoniously before the mud had time to get any grip upon him. Pausing for a moment to scrutinize the oozy expanse, she thrust the little animal furiously along to the left, searching for a safe passage. Before she could find one, however, the tide was upon them, their feet splashing in the thin yellow wavelets.

A broken soap-box, tossed overboard from some ship, came washing up, and stranded just before them. With a whimper of delight, as if he thought the box a safe refuge, the cub scrambled upon it; but his mother ruthlessly tumbled him off and hustled him onward, floundering and splashing.

"Ye'll hev to swim fer it, Old Woman!" growled the now excited watcher behind the pine-tree on the cliff.

As the creeping flood by this time overspread the ooze for a couple of yards ahead of them, the mother could no longer discriminate as to what lay beneath it. She could do nothing now but dash ahead blindly. Catching up the cub between her jaws, in a grip that made him squeal, she launched herself straight toward shore, hardly daring to let her feet rest an instant where they touched. Fortune favoured her in this rush. She got ahead of the tide. She gained upon it, perhaps twice her body's length. Then she paused, to drop the cub. But the pause was fatal. She began to sink instantly. She had come upon a "honey-pot" of stiffer consistency than the rest, which had sustained her while she was in swift motion, but now, in return for that support, clutched her in a grip the more inexorable. With all her huge strength she strained to wrench herself clear. But in vain. She had no purchase. There was nothing to put forth her strength upon. In her terror and despair she squealed aloud, with her snout high in air as if appealing to the blank, blue, empty sky. The cub, terror-stricken, strove to clamber upon her back.

That harsh cry of hers, however, was but the outburst of one moment's weakness. The next moment the indomitable old bear was striving silently and systematically to release herself. She would wrench one great fore arm clear, lift it high, and feel about for a solid foundation beneath the ooze. Failing in this, she would yield that paw to the enemy again, tear the other loose, and feel about for a foothold in another direction. At the same time she drew out her body to its full length, and lay flat, so that she might gain as much support as possible by distributing her weight. Because of this sagacity, and because the mire at this point had more substance than in most of the other "honey-pots," she made a good fight, and almost, but not quite, held her own. By the time the tide had once more overtaken her she had sunk but a little way, and was still far from giving up the unequal struggle.

Yet for all the great beast's strength, and valour, and devotion, there could have been but one end to that brave battle, and mother and cub would have disappeared, in a few minutes more, under the stealthy, whispering onrush of the flood, had not the whimsical Providence--or Hazard--of the Wild come curiously to their aid. Among the jetsam of those restless Fundy tides almost anything that will float may appear, from a matchbox to a barn. What appeared just now was a big spruce log, escaped from the boom on some river emptying into the bay. It came softly wallowing in, lipped by the little waves, and passed close by the nose of the old bear, where she struggled with the water up to her shoulders.

Quick as thought she flashed up a heavy paw, caught the log by one end, and pulled the butt under her chest. The purchase thus gained enabled her to free the other paw--and in a few seconds more the weight of the fore part of her body was on the end of the log, forcing it down to the mud. Greedy as that mud was, it was yet incapable of engulfing a full-grown spruce timber quickly enough to defeat the bear's purpose. Stretching far forward on the submerged log, she strained her muscles to their utmost, and slowly drew her hind quarters free from the deadly grip that held them. Then, seizing in her jaws the cub, which was swimming and whimpering beside her, she carefully felt her way farther along the log, and sat down upon it to rest, clutching the youngster closely in one great fore arm.

Not till the tide had risen nearly to her neck did the mother move again. She was recovering her strength. Utterly daunted by the peril of the "honey-pots," she chose rather to trust the tide itself. At last, catching the cub again by the back of the neck, she swam for the shore. The tide was now within a couple of hundred yards from the bases of the cliffs, and lapping upon solid, sun-baked clay. The strong flood helping her, she swam fast, though laboriously by reason of the burden in her teeth. Soon her hinder feet struck ground--but she was afraid to trust it, and nervously drew them up beneath her. A few moments more and she felt undeniably firm footing; whereupon she plunged forward with a rush, and never paused, even to drop the squirming cub, till she was above high-water mark.

When, at last, she set the little beast down, she was in such a hurry to get away from the shore and back into the secure green woods that she would not trust him to follow her, as usual, but drove him on ahead, as fast as he could move, toward the cleft in the cliffs. As they turned up the rugged trail her haste relaxed, and she went more slowly, but still driving the cub ahead of her, that she might be quite sure that the "honey-pots" would not reach up and clutch at him again.

As the muddy, weary, bedraggled, pathetic-looking pair passed within tempting range of the pine-tree on the cliff-top, the woodsman instinctively threw forward his rifle. But the next moment he dropped it, with a slight flush, and gave a quick glance around him as if he feared that unseen eyes might have taken note of the gesture.

"Hell!" he muttered, "I'd 'a' been no better'n a murderer, 'f I'd 'a' gone an' plugged the Old Girl now!"

THE FIGHT AT THE WALLOW

I

FAR to the northeast of Ringwaak Hill, just beyond that deep, far-rimmed lake which begets the torrent of the Ottanoonsis, rise the bluff twin summits of Old Walquitch, presiding over an unbroken and almost untrodden wilderness. Some way up the southeasterly flank of the loftier and more butting of the twin peaks ran a vast, open shelf, or terrace, a kind of barren, whose swampy but austere soil bore no growth but wiry bush. The green tips of this bushy growth were a favoured "browse" of the caribou, who, though no lovers of the heights, would often wander up from their shaggy and austere plains in quest of this aromatic forage. But this lofty mountainside barren had yet another attraction for the caribou. Close at its edge, just where a granite buttress fell away steeply toward the lake, a tiny, almost imperceptible spring, stained with iron and pungent with salt, trickled out from among the roots of a dense, low thicket. Past the bare spot made by these oozings, and round behind the thicket, led a dim trail, worn by the feet of caribou, moose, bear, deer, and other stealthy wayfarers. And to this spring, when the moon of the falling leaves brought in the season of love and war, the caribou bulls were wont to come, delighting to form their wallow in the pungent, salty mud.

The bald twin peaks of Old Walquitch were ghostly white in the flood of the full moon, just risen, and swimming like a globe of witch's fire over the far, dark, wooded horizon. But the bushy shelf and the spring by the thicket, were still in shadow. Along the trail to the spring, moving noiselessly, yet with a confident dignity, came a paler shadow, the shape of a huge, gray-white caribou bull with wide-spreading antlers.

At the edge of the spring the bull stopped and began sniffing the sharp-scented mud. Apparently he found no sign of a rival having passed that way before him, or of a cow having kept tryst there. Lifting his splendid head he stared all about him in the shadow, and up at the bare, illuminated fronts of the twin peaks.

As the light spread down the mountain to the edge of the shelf, and the moon rose into his view, he "belled" harshly several times across the dark wastes outspread below him.

Receiving no answer to his defiance, the great bull turned his attention again to the ooze around the spring. After sniffing it all over he fell to furrowing it excitedly with the two lowermost branches of his antlers,--short, broad, palmated projections thrust out low over his forehead, and called by woodsmen "the ploughs." Every few seconds he would toss his head fiercely, like an ordinary bull, and throw the ooze over his shoulders. Then he pawed the cool, strong-smelling stuff to what he seemed to consider a fitting consistency, sniffed it over again, and raised his head to "bell" a fresh challenge across the spacious solitudes. Receiving no answer, he snorted in disgust, flung himself down on the trampled ooze, and began to wallow with a sort of slow and intense vehemence, grunting massively from time to time with volcanic emotion.

The wallow was now in the full flood of the moonlight. In that mysterious illumination the caribou, encased in shining ooze, took on the grotesque and enormous aspect of some monster of the prediluvian slimes. Suddenly his wallowing stopped, and his antlers, dripping mud, were lifted erect. For a few moments he was motionless as a rock, listening. He had caught the snapping of a twig, in the trail below the edge of the shelf. The sound was repeated; and he understood. Blowing smartly, as if to clear the mud from about his nostrils, he lurched to his feet, stalked forth from the wallow, and stood staring arrogantly along the trail by which he had come. The next moment another pair of antlers appeared; and then another bull, tall but lean, and with long, spiky, narrow horns, mounted over the edge of the shelf, and halted to eye the apparition before him.

The newcomer was of a darker hue than the lord of the wallow, and of much slimmer build,--altogether less formidable in appearance. But he looked very fit and fearless as, after a moment's supercilious survey of his rival's ooze-dripping form, he came mincing forward to the attack. The two, probably, had never seen each other before; but in rutting season all caribou bulls are enemies at sight.

The white bull--no longer white now, but black and silver in the moonlight--stood for some seconds quite motionless, his head low, his broad and massive antlers thrust forward, his feet planted firmly and apart. Ominous in his stillness, he waited till his light-stepping and debonair adversary was within twenty feet of him. Then, with an explosive blowing through his nostrils, he launched himself forward to the attack.

Following the customary tactics of his kind, the second bull lowered his antlers to receive the charge. But in the last fraction of a breath before the crash, he changed his mind. Leaping aside with a lightning alertness more like the action of a red buck than that of a caribou, he just evaded the shock. At the same time two of the spiky prongs of one antler ripped a long gash down his opponent's flank.

Amazed at this departure from the usual caribou tactics, and smarting with the anguish of that punishing stroke, the white bull whirled in his tracks, and charged again, blind with fury. The slim stranger had already turned, and awaited him again, with lowered antlers in readiness, close by the edge of the wallow. This time he seemed determined to meet the shock squarely according to the rules of the game--which apparently demand that the prowess of a caribou bull shall be determined by his pushing power. But again he avoided, leaping aside as if on springs; and again his sharp prongs furrowed his enemy's flank. With a grunt of rage the latter plunged on into the wallow, where he slipped forward upon his knees.

Had the newcomer been a little more resourceful he might now have taken his adversary at a terrible disadvantage, and won an easy victory. But he hesitated, being too much enamoured of his own method of fighting; and in the moment of hesitation opportunity passed him by. The white bull, recovering himself with suddenly awakened agility, was on his feet and on guard again in an instant.

These two disastrous experiences, however, had added wariness and wisdom to the great bull's fighting rage. His wound, his momentary discomfiture, had opened his arrogant eyes to the fact that his antagonist was a dangerous one. He stood vigilant and considering for a few seconds, no longer with his feet planted massively for a resistless rush, but balanced, and all his forces gathered well in hand; while his elusive foe stepped lightly and tauntingly from side to side before him, threateningly.

When the white bull made up his mind to attack again, instead of charging madly to swab his foe off the earth, he moved forward at a brisk stride, ready to check himself on the instant and block the enemy's side stroke. Within a couple of yards of his opponent he stopped short. The latter stood motionless, antlers lowered as before, apparently quite willing to lock horns. But the white bull would not be lured into a rush. Fiercely impatient he stamped the ground with a broad, clacking forehoof.

Just at this moment, as if in response to the challenge of the hoof, the stranger charged like lightning. But almost in the same motion he swerved aside, seeking again to catch his adversary on the flank. Swift and cunning as he was, however, the white bull was this time all readiness. He whirled, head down. With a sharp, dry crash the two sets of antlers came together, and locked.

That this should have happened was the irremediable mistake of the slim stranger. In that close encounter, fury against fury, force against force fairly pitted, his speed and his agility counted for nothing. For a few seconds, indeed, in sheer desperation he succeeded in withstanding his heavier and more powerful foe. With hind feet braced far back, haunches strained, flank heaving and quivering, the two held steady, staccato grunts and snorts attesting the ferocity of their efforts. Then the hind foot of the younger bull slipped a little. With a convulsive wrench he recovered his footing; and again the struggle hung at poise. But it was only for a few moments. Suddenly, as if he had felt his opportunity approach, the white bull threw all his strength into a mightier thrust. The legs of his adversary seemed to crumple up like paper beneath him.

This would have been the end of the young bull's battlings and wooings; but as his good luck would have it, it was at the very edge of the shelf that he collapsed. Disengaging his victorious antlers, the conqueror thrust viciously and evisceratingly at the victim's exposed flank. The latter was just struggling to rise, with precarious foothold on the loose-turfed brink of the steep. As he writhed away wildly from the goring points, the bushes and turf crumbled away, and he fell backwards, rolling and crashing till he brought up, battered but whole, in a sturdy thicket of young firs. Regaining his feet he slunk off hurriedly into the dark of the woods. And the victor, standing on the brink in the white glare of the moonlight, "belled" his triumph hoarsely across the solemn spaces of the night.

II

A sound of footfalls, hesitating but apparently making no attempt at concealment, came from the bend of the trail beyond the wallow; and the great white bull wheeled savagely to see what was approaching. As he glared, however, the angry ridge of hair cresting his neck sank amiably. A young cow, attracted by his calls and the noise of the battle, was coming around the thicket.

At the edge of the thicket, not a dozen paces from the black ooze-bed of the wallow, the cow paused coyly, as if doubtful of her welcome. She murmured in her throat, a sort of rough allurement which seemed to the white bull's ears extraordinarily enticing. He answered, very softly, and stepped forward a pace or two, inviting rather than pursuing. Reassured, the young cow advanced confidently and eagerly to meet him.

At this moment, out from the heart of the thicket plunged a towering black form, with wide, snarling jaw's agleam in the moonlight. It seemed to launch itself through the air, as if from a height. One great, taloned paw struck the young cow full on the neck, a crashing blow, shattering the vertebrae through all their armour of muscle. With a groan the stricken cow sank down, her outstretched muzzle smothered in the ooze of the wallow; and the monstrous bulk of the bear fell upon her, tearing the warm flesh hungrily.

In ninety-nine cases out of a hundred, the most hot-headed and powerful bull of the caribou will shrink from trying conclusions with a full grown black bear. The duel, as a rule, is too cruelly one-sided. The bear, on the other hand, knows that a courageous bull is no easy victim; and the monster ambuscaded in the thicket had been waiting for one or both of the rivals to be disabled before making his attack. The approach of the young cow had been an unexpected favour of the Powers that order the wilderness; and in clutching his opportunity he had scornfully and absolutely put the white bull out of the reckoning.

But this bull was the exceptional one, the one that confounds generalizations, and confirms the final supremacy of the unexpected. He was altogether fearless, indifferent to odds, and just now flushed with overwhelming victory. Moreover, he was aflame with mating ardour; and the mate of his desire had just been brutally struck down before his eyes. For a moment or two he stood bewildered, not daunted, but amazed by the terrific apparition and the appalling event. Then a mad fire raged through all his veins, his great muscles swelled, the stiff hair on his neck and shoulders stood straight up, his eyes went crimson--and without a sound he charged across the wallow.

When the bulls of the caribou kin fight each other, the weapons of their sole dependence are their antlers. But when they fight alien enemies they are wont to hold their heads high and strike with the battering, knife-edged weapons of their fore-hoofs. The bear, crouched upon his quivering prey, was too absorbed and too scornful to look for any assault. The bull was upon him, therefore, before he had time to guard his exposed flank. From the corner of his eye, he saw a big glistening shape which reared suddenly above him, and, clever boxer that he was, he threw up a ponderous forearm to parry the blow. But he was too late. With all the force of some seven hundred pounds of rage, avenging rage, behind him, these great hoofs, with their cutting edges, came down upon his side, smashing in several ribs, and gashing a wide wound down into his loins. The shock was so terrific that his own counter stroke, usually so swift and unerring, went wild altogether, and he was sent rolling clear of the body of his prey.

Instantly upon delivering his stroke, the white bull had pranced lightly aside, knowing well enough the swift and deadly effectiveness of a bear's paw. But he struck yet again, almost, it seemed, in the same breath, and just as the bear was struggling up upon his haunches. Frantically, out of his astonishment, fury, and pain, the bear attempted to guard. He succeeded, indeed, in warding off those deadly hoofs from his flank; but he caught an almost disabling blow on the point of the left shoulder, putting his left forearm out of business. With a squawling grunt he swung about upon his haunches, bringing his right toward the enemy, and sat up, savagely but anxiously defensive.

Sore wounded though he was, the bear was not yet beaten. One fair buffet of his right paw, could he but land it in the proper place,--on nose, or neck, or leg--might yet give him the victory, and let him crawl off to nurse his hurts in some dense covert, leaving his broken foe to die in the wallow. But the white bull, though he had underrated his former antagonist, was in no danger of misprizing this one. He was now as wary as he had, in the previous case, been rash. Moreover, he had had a dreadful object lesson in the power of the bear's paw. The body of the cow before him kept him from forgetting.

Stepping restlessly from side to side, threatening now with hoof and now with antlers, he seemed each instant upon the point of a fresh attack; and the bear, with swaying muzzle and blazing, shifting eyes, kept following his every motion. Again and again he gathered his muscles for a fresh charge--but each time he checked himself with a realization that the body of the slain cow was exactly in his way, hampering his avoidance of a counter-stroke.

After some minutes of this feinting, the caribou stood still, deliberating some new move. Instantly the bear, also, became motionless as a stone. The sudden peace was like a shock of enchantment, a violent sorcery, and over it the blue-white, flooding shine of the moonlight seemed to take on some sinister significance. The seconds lengthened out as a nightmare, till at last the stupendous stillness was broken by the wild clamour of a loon, far down on the lake. As the distant cry shrilled up the mountainside, the white bull stirred, shook his antlers, and blew loudly through his nostril. It was a note of challenge--but in it the bear divined a growing hesitancy. Perhaps, after all, this fight, which had gone so sorely against him, might not have to be fought out! He dropped, whirled about so quietly one could hardly follow the motion--and in a flash was up again on his haunches, right paw uplifted, eyes blazing vigilant defiance. But he had retreated several feet in that swift manoeuvre! His move was a confusion of defeat--but his attitude was a warning that he was dangerous in defeat. The bull followed, but only for a couple of steps, which brought him so that he bestrode the body of the cow. Here he halted, still threatening; and again the two confronted each other motionlessly.

This time, however, the spell was broken by the bear himself. Suddenly he repeated his former manoeuvre; and again turned to face his adversary. But the bull did not follow. Without a movement he stood, as if content with his victory. And after a few moments the bear, as if realizing that the fight was over, flung himself aside from the trail and went limping off painfully through the bushes, keeping a watchful eye over his shoulder till he vanished into a bunch of dense spruce against the mountainside.

The white bull eyed his going proudly. Then he looked down at the torn and lifeless body between his feet. He had not really taken note of it before. Now he bent his head and sniffed at it with wondering interrogation. The spreading blood, still warm, smote his nostrils; and all at once, it seemed, death and the fear of death were borne in upon his arrogant heart. He tossed his head, snorting wildly, flung himself clear of the uncomprehended, dreadful thing upon the ground, bounded over the wallow as if it, too, had grown terrifying, and fled away up the trail through the merciless, unconcealing moonlight, till he reached the end of the open shelf and a black wood hid his sudden fear of the unknown.

Sonny and the Kid

THE little old gray house, with its gray barn and low wagon shed, stood in the full sun at the top of a gullied and stony lane. Behind it the ancient forest, spruce and fir and hemlock, came down and brooded darkly over the edge of the rough, stump-strewn pasture. The lane, leading up to the house from the main road, climbed between a sloping buckwheat field on the one hand and a buttercupped meadow on the other. On either side of the lane, cutting it off from the fields, straggled a zigzag snake fence, with milk-weed, tansy, and mullein growing raggedly in its corners.

At the head of the lane, where it came out upon the untidy but homely looking yard, stood a largish black and tan dog, his head on one side, his ears cocked, his short stub of a tail sticking out straight and motionless, tense with expectation. He was staring at a wagon which came slowly along the main road, drawn by a jogging, white-faced sorrel. The expression in the dog's eyes was that of a hope so eager that nothing but absolute certainty could permit him to believe in its approaching fulfilment. His mouth was half open, as if struggling to aid his vision.

He was an odd looking beast, formidable in his sturdy strength and his massiveness of jaw; and ugly beyond question, but for the alert intelligence of his eyes. A palpable mongrel, he showed none the less that he had strains of distinction in his ancestry. English bull was the blood most clearly proclaimed, in his great chest, short, crooked legs, fine coat, and square, powerful head. His pronounced black and tan seemed to betray some beagle kinship, as did his long, close-haired ears. Whoever had docked his tail, in his defenceless puppyhood, had evidently been too tender-hearted to cut those silken and sensitive ears. So Sonny had been obliged to face life in the incongruous garb of short tail and long ears--which is almost as unpardonable as yellow shoes with a top hat.

When the wagon drew close to the foot of the lane, Sonny was still uncertain. There might be other white faced sorrels than lazy old Bill. The man in the wagon certainly looked like his beloved master, Joe Barnes; but Joe Barnes was always alone on the wagon-seat, while this man had a child beside him, a child with long, bright, yellow hair and a little red cap. This to Sonny was a bewildering phenomenon. But when at last the wagon turned up the lane, his doubts were finally resolved. His stub of a tail jerked spasmodically, in its struggle to wag. Then with two or three delirious yelps of joy he started madly down the lane. At the sound of his voice the door of the gray house opened. A tall, thin woman in a bluish homespun skirt and red calico waist came out, and moved slowly across the yard to welcome the new arrivals.

When Sonny, yelping and dancing, met the creaking wagon as it bumped its way upward over the gullies, his master greeted him with a "Hello, Sonny!" as usual; but to the dog's quick perception there was a difference in his tone, a difference that was almost an indifference. Joe Barnes was absorbed. At other times, he was wont to seem warmly interested in Sonny's welcoming antics, and would keep up a running fire of talk with him while the old sorrel plodded up the lane. To-day, however, Joe's attention was occupied by the yellow-haired child beside him; and Sonny's demonstrations, he knew not why, became perceptibly less ecstatic. It was of no consequence whatever to him that the child stared at him with dancing eyes and cried delightedly, "Oh, Unc' Joe, what a pretty doggie! Oh, what a nice doggie! Can I have him, Unc' Joe?"

"All right, Kid," said Joe Barnes, gazing down adoringly upon the little red cap; "he's yourn. His name's Sonny, an' he's the best dawg ever chased a chipmunk. He'll love ye, Kid, most as much as yer old Unc' Joe an' Aunt Ann does."

When the yard was reached, the tall woman in the red calico waist was at the side of the wagon before the driver's "Whoa!" brought the horse to a stop. The little one was snatched down from the seat and hugged vehemently to her heart.

"Poor lamb! Precious lamb!" she murmured. "I'll be a mother to you, please God!"

"I want my mummie! Where's she gone to?" cried the child, suddenly reminded of a loss which he was beginning to forget. But his aunt changed the subject hastily.

"Ain't he the livin' image of Jim?" she demanded in a voice of wondering admiration. "Did ever you see the likes of it, father?"

Under the pretence of examining him more critically, Joe took the child into his own arms, and looked at him with ardent eyes. "Yes," said he, "the Kid does favour Jim, more'n his--" But he checked himself at the word. "An' he's a regular little man too!" he went on. "Come all the way up on the cars by himself, an' wasn't a mite o' trouble, the conductor said."

Utterly engrossed in the little one, neither Joe nor his wife gave a look or a thought to Sonny, who was leaping upon them joyously. For years he had been almost the one centre of attention for the childless couple, who had treated him as a child, caressing him, spoiling him, and teaching him to feel his devotion necessary to them. Now, finding himself quite ignored, he quieted down all at once and stood for a few seconds gazing reproachfully at the scene. The intimacy with Joe and Ann which he had so long enjoyed had developed almost a human quality in his intelligence and his feelings. Plainly, now, he was forgotten. His master and mistress had withdrawn their love and were pouring it out upon this stranger child. His ears and stub tail drooping in misery, he turned away, walked sorrowfully over to the horse, and sniffed at the latter's nose as if to beg for some explanation of what had happened. But the old sorrel, pleasantly occupied in cropping at the short, sweet grass behind the well, had neither explanation nor sympathy to offer. Sonny went off to his kennel, a place he scorned to notice, as a rule, because the best in the house had hitherto been held none too good for him. Creeping in with a beaten air, he lay down with his nose on his paws in the doorway, and tried to understand what had come upon him. One thing only was quite clear to him. It was all the fault of the child with the yellow curls.

Sonny had had no experience with children. The few he had met he had regarded with that impersonal benevolence which was his attitude toward all humanity. His formidable appearance had saved him from finding out that humanity could be cruel and brutal. So now, in his unhappiness, he had no jealous anger. He simply wanted to keep away from this small being who had caused his hurt.

But even this grace was not to be allowed him. By the time Joe Barnes and Ann, both trying to hold the little one in their arms at the same time, had made their impeded way to the house, the little one had begun to find their ardour a shade embarrassing. To him there were lots of things better than being hugged and kissed. This shining green backwoods world was quite new to his city born eyes, and he wanted to find out all about it, at once, for himself. He began struggling vigorously to get down out of the imprisoning arms.

"Put me down, Unc' Joe!" he demanded. "I want to play with my doggie."

"All right, Kid," responded Joe, complying instantly. "Here Sonny, Sonny, come an' git acquainted with the Kid!"

"Yes, come and see the Kid, Sonny!" re 惟 hoed the woman, devouring the little yellow head with her eyes. His real name was Alfred, but Joe had called him "the Kid," and that was to be his appellation thenceforth.

Hearing his name called, Sonny emerged from his kennel and came forward, but not with his wonted eagerness. Very soberly, but with prompt obedience he came, and thrust his massive head under Joe's hand for the accustomed caress. But the caress was not forthcoming. Joe simply forgot it, so absorbed was he, his gaunt, weather-beaten face glowing and melting with smiles as he gazed at the child.

"Here's your dawg, Kid!" said he, and watched delightedly to see how the little one would go about asserting proprietorship.

The woman was the more subtle of the two in her sympathies. "Sonny," she said, pulling the dog forward, "here's the Kid, yer little master. See you mind what he tells you, and see you take good keer o' him."

Sonny wagged his tail obediently, his load of misery lightening under the touch of his mistress's hand. He leaned against her knees, comforted for a moment, though his love was more for the man than for her. But he would not look at the Kid. He shut his eyes with an expression of endurance as the little one's hand patted him vehemently on the face, and his stub tail stopped wagging. In a dim way he recognized that he must not be uncivil to this small stranger who had so instantaneously and completely usurped his place. But beyond this he could think of nothing but his master, who had grown indifferent. Suddenly, with a burst of longing for reconciliation, he jerked abruptly away from the child's hands, wriggled in between Joe's legs, and strove to climb up and lick his face.

At the look of disappointment which passed over the child's face Joe Barnes felt a sudden rush of anger. Stupidly misunderstanding, he thought that Sonny was merely trying to avoid the child. He straightened up his tall figure, snatched the little one to his breast, and exclaimed in a harsh voice, "If ye can't be nice to the Kid, git out!"

The words "Git out!" with the tone in which they were uttered, would have been comprehensible to a much meaner intelligence than Sonny's. As if he had been whipped, he curled down his abbreviated tail, and ran and hid himself in his kennel.

"Sonny didn't mean to be ugly to the Kid, father," protested Ann, "He jest don't quite understand the situation yet, an' he's wonderin' why ye don't make so much of him as ye used to. I don't blame him fer feelin' a leetle mite left out in the cold."

Joe felt a vague suspicion that Ann might be right; but it was a very vague suspicion, just enough to make him feel uneasy and put him on the defensive. Being obstinate and something of a crank, this only added heat to his irritation. "I ain't got no use fer any dawg that don't know enough to take to a kid on sight!" he declared, readjusting the little red cap on the child's curls.

"Of course, father," acquiesced Ann discreetly; "but you'll find Sonny'll be all right."

Here the child, who had been squirming with impatience, piped up, "I want to go an' see my doggie in his little house!" he declared.

"Oh, no, Kid, we're goin' to let Sonny be fer a bit. We're goin' to see the calf, the pretty black an' white calf, round back o' the barn, now. You go along with Aunty Ann while I onhitch old Bill. An' then we'll all go an' see the little pigs."

His mind altogether diverted by the suggestion of such strange delights, the little fellow trotted off joyously with Ann, while Joe Barnes led the old sorrel to the barn, grumbling to himself at what he chose to call Sonny's "ugliness" in not making friends with the Kid.

* * * * *

From that hour Sonny's life was changed. In fact, it seemed to him no longer life at all. His master's indifference grew swiftly to an unreasoning anger against him; and as he fretted over it continually, a malicious fate seemed to delight in putting him, or leading him to put himself, ever in the wrong. Absorbed in longing for his master, he hardly thought of the child at all. Several times, in a blundering effort to make things right with Sonny and the Kid, Joe seated himself on the back doorstep, took the little one on his knee, and called Sonny to come and make friends. At the sound of the loved summons Sonny shot out from the kennel, which had become his constant refuge, tore wildly across the yard, and strove, in a sort of ecstasy, to show his forgiveness and his joy by climbing into Joe's lap. Being a large dog, and the lap already filled, this meant roughly crowding out the Kid, of whose very existence, at this moment, Sonny was unaware. But to the obtuse man Sonny's action seemed nothing more than a mean and jealous effort to supplant the Kid.

To the Kid this proceeding of Sonny's was a fine game. He would grapple with the dog, hug him, pound him gleefully with his little fists, and call him every pet name he knew.

But the man would rise to his feet angrily, and cry, "If that's all ye're good fer, git! Git out, I tell ye!" And Sonny, heartsore and bewildered, would shrink back hopelessly to his kennel. When this, or something much like it, had happened several times, even Ann, for all her finer perceptions, began to feel that Sonny might be a bit nicer to the Kid, and, as a consequence, to stint her kindness. But to Sonny, sunk in his misery and pining only for that love which his master had so inexplicably withdrawn from him, it mattered little whether Ann was neglectful or not.

Uneventfully day followed day on the lonely backwoods farm. To Sonny, the discarded, the discredited, they were all hopeless days, dark and interminable. But to the Kid they were days of wonder, every one. He loved the queer black and white pigs, which he studied intently through the cracks in the boarding of their pen. He loved the calf, and the three velvet-eyed cows, and the two big red oxen, inseparable yoke fellows. The chickens were an inexhaustible interest to him; and so were the airy throngs of buttercups afloat on the grass, and the yet more aerial troops of the butterflies flickering above them, white and brown and red and black and gold and yellow and maroon. But in the last choice he loved best of all the silent, unresponsive Sonny, of whose indifference he seemed quite unaware. Sonny, lying on the grass, would look at him soberly, submit to his endearments without one answering wag of the tail, and at last, after the utmost patience that courtesy could require, would slowly get up, yawn, and stroll off to his kennel or to some pretended business behind the barn. His big heart harboured no resentment against the child, whom he knew to be a child and irresponsible. His resentment was all against fate, or life, or whatever it was, the vague, implacable force which was causing Joe Barnes to hurt him. For Joe Barnes he had only sorrow and hungry devotion.

Little by little, however, Sonny's lonely and sorrowful heart, in spite of itself, was beginning to warm toward the unconscious child. Though still outwardly indifferent, he began to feel gratified rather than bored when the Kid came up and gaily disturbed his slumbers by pounding him on the head with his little palm and tumbling over his sturdy back. It was a mild gratification, however, and seemed to call for no demonstrative expression.

Then, one noon, he chanced to be lying, heavy-hearted, some ten or a dozen paces in front of the kitchen door, while Joe Barnes sat on the doorstep smoking his after-dinner pipe, and Ann bustled through the dish washing. At such times, in the old happy days, Sonny's place had always been at Joe Barnes's feet; but those times seemed to have been forgotten by Joe Barnes, who had the Kid beside him. Suddenly, tired of sitting still, the little one jumped up and ran over to Sonny. Sonny resolutely pretended to be asleep. Laughingly the child sprawled over him, pulled his ears gently, then tried to push open his eyes. A little burst of warmth gushed up in Sonny's sad heart. With a swift impulse he lifted his muzzle and licked the Kid, a generous, ample lick across the face.

Alas! as blundering fate would have it, the Kid's face was closer than Sonny had imagined. He not only licked it, but at the same time bumped it violently with his wet muzzle. Taken by surprise and half-dazed, the Kid drew back with a sharp little "Oh!" His eyes grew very wide, and for an instant his mouth quivered as if he was going to cry. This was all Joe Barnes saw. Springing to his feet, with a smothered oath, he ran, caught the Kid up in his arms, and gave Sonny a fierce kick in the ribs which sent him rushing back to his kennel with a howl of grief and pain.

Ann had come running from the house in amazement. The Kid was sobbing, and struggling to get down from Joe's arms.

Ann snatched him away anxiously. "What did Sonny do to ye, the bad dawg!" she demanded.

"He ain't bad. He's good. He jest kissed me too hard!" protested the little one indignantly.

"He hurt the Kid's face. I ain't right sure but what he snapped at him," said Joe Barnes.

"He didn't hurt me! He didn't mean to," went on the Kid.

"Of course he didn't," said Ann with conviction. "Father, ye're too hard on the dawg. Ye hadn't oughter have kicked him."

An obstinate look settled on Joe Barnes's face. "Yes, I had, too. 'N' he'll be gittin' more'n that, ef he don't l'arn not to be ugly to the Kid," he retorted harshly. Then, with an uneasy sense that, whether right or wrong, he was in the minority, he returned to the doorstep and moodily resumed his smoking. Ann called Sonny many times to come out and get his dinner. But Sonny, broken-hearted, and the ruins of all his life and love and trust tumbled about his ears, would not hear her. He was huddled in the back of his kennel, with his nose jammed down into the corner.

* * * * *

Two days later it happened that both Joe and Ann went down together into the field in front of the house to weed the carrot patch. They left the Kid asleep in his trundle bed, in the little room off the kitchen. When they were gone, Sonny came out of his kennel and lay down in the middle of the yard, where he could keep a watchful eye on everything belonging to Joe Barnes.

It was the Kid's invariable custom to sleep soundly for a good two hours of the early afternoon. On this afternoon, however, he broke his custom. Joe and Ann had not been ten minutes away, when he appeared in the kitchen door, his yellow hair tousled, his cheeks rosy, his plump fists trying to rub the sleep out of his eyes. His face was aggrieved, because he had woke up and found himself alone. But at the sight of Sonny the grievance was forgotten. He ran to the dog and began to maul him joyously.

His recent bitter experience raw in his heart, Sonny did not dare to respond, but lay with his nose on his paws, unstirring, while the child sprawled over him. After a few minutes this utter unresponsiveness chilled even the Kid's enthusiasm. He jumped up and cast his eyes about in search of some diversion more exciting. His glance wandered out past the barn and up the pasture toward the edge of the forest. A squirrel, sitting on a black stump in the pasture, suddenly began jumping about and shrilly chattering. This was something quite new and very interesting. The Kid crawled through the bars and started up the pasture as fast as his sturdy little legs could carry him.

The squirrel saw him coming, but knowing very well that he was not dangerous, held his ground, bouncing up and down on the stump in vociferous excitement. When the Kid was within three feet of him, he gave a wild "K-r-r-r-r!" of derision, and sprang to another stump. With eyes dancing and eager little hands outstretched, the Kid followed--again and again, and yet again--till he was led to the very edge of the wood. Then the mocking imp in red fur whisked up an ancient hemlock, and hid himself, in silence, in a high crotch, tired of the game.

At the edge of the woods the Kid stopped, peering in among the shadows with mingled curiosity and awe. The bright patches of sunlight on the brown forest floor and on the scattered underbrush allured him. Presently, standing out in conspicuous isolation, a great crimson toadstool caught his eye. He wanted the beautiful thing intensely, to play with. But he was afraid. Leaning his face against the old fence, he gazed through desirously. But the silence made him more and more afraid. If only the squirrel would come back and play with him, he would not be afraid. He was on the point of giving up the beautiful crimson toadstool and turning back home, when he saw a little gray bird hopping amid the lower limbs of a spruce in among the shadows. "Tsic-a-dee-dee!" whistled the little gray bird, blithely and reassuringly. At once the shadows and the stillness lost their terrors. The Kid squeezed boldly through the fence and started in for the glowing toadstool.

Just as he reached the coloured thing and stooped to seize it, a sharp "Tzip, tzip!" and a rustling of stiff feathers startled him. Looking up, he saw a bright-eyed brown bird running hither and thither before him, trailing one wing on the ground as if unable to fly. It was such a pretty bird! And it seemed so tame! The Kid felt sure he could catch it. Grabbing up the crimson toadstool, and holding it clutched to his bosom with one hand, he ran eagerly after the brown bird. The bird, a wily old hen partridge, bent on leading the intruder away from her hidden brood, kept fluttering laboriously on just beyond his reach, till she came to a dense patch of underbrush. She was just about to dive into this thicket, when she leaped into the air, instead, with a frightened squawk, and whirred up into the branches of a lofty birch near by.

Bitterly disappointed, the Kid gazed up after her, still clutching the bright toadstool to his breast. Then, by instinct rather than by reason, he dropped his eyes to the thicket, and stared in to see what had frightened away the pretty brown bird.

At first he could see nothing. But to his sensitive little nerves came a feeling that something was there. Gradually his eyes, accustoming themselves to the gloom, began to disentangle substance and shadow. Then suddenly he detected the form of a gray crouching animal. He saw its tufted ears, its big round face, with mouth half open grinningly. Its great, round, pale, yellow green eyes were staring straight at him.

In his fright the Kid dropped his toadstool and stared back at the gray animal. His first impulse was to turn and run; but, somehow, he was afraid to do that--afraid to turn his back on the pale-eyed, crouching shape. As he gazed, trembling, he saw that the animal looked like a huge gray cat.

At this thought he felt a trifle reassured. Cats were kind, and nice to play with. A big cat wouldn't hurt him, he felt quite sure of that. But when, after a minute or two of moveless glaring, the big cat, never taking its round eyes from his face, began to creep straight toward him, stealthily, without a sound, then his terror all came back. In the extremity of his fear he burst out crying, not very loud, but softly and pitifully, as if he hardly knew what he was doing. His little hands hanging straight down at his sides, his head bent slightly forward, he stood helplessly staring at this strange, terrible cat creeping toward him through the thicket.

* * * * *

Sonny, meanwhile, had grown uneasy the moment the Kid climbed through the bars into the pasture. The Kid had never gone into the pasture before. Sonny got up, turned round, and lay down in such a position that he could see just what the child was doing. He knew the little one belonged to Joe Barnes; and he could not let anything belonging to Joe Barnes get lost or run away. When the Kid reached the edge of the woods and stood looking through the fence, then Sonny roused himself, and started up the pasture in a leisurely, indifferent way, as if it was purely his own whim that took him in that direction. He pretended not to see the Kid at all. But in reality he was watching, with an anxious intentness, every move the little one made. He was determined to do his duty by Joe Barnes.

But when at last the Kid wriggled through the fence and darted into the gloom of the forest, Sonny's solicitude became more personal. He knew that the forest was a place of many strange perils. It was no place for the Kid. A sudden fear seized him at thought of what might happen to the Kid, there in the great and silent shadows. He broke into a frantic run, scrambled through the fence, picked up the little adventurer's trail, and darted onward till he caught sight of the Kid's bright curly head, apparently intent on gazing into a thicket. At the sight he stopped abruptly, then sauntered forward with a careless air, as if it was the most ordinary chance in the world that he should come across the Kid, away off here alone.

Instinctively, under the subtle influence of the forest silence, Sonny went forward softly, on his toes, though anything like stealth was altogether foreign to him. As he crept up, he wondered what it was in the thicket to keep him so still. There was something mysterious about it. The hair began to rise along Sonny's back. Then, a moment later, he heard the Kid crying. There was no mistaking the note of terror in that hopeless, helpless little sound. Sonny did not need to reason about it; his heart understood all that was necessary. Something was frightening the Kid. His white teeth bared themselves, and he darted forward.

At this instant there came a crackling and swishing in the thicket; and the Kid, as if released from a spell, turned with a scream and started to flee. He tripped on a root, however, and fell headlong on his face, his yellow curls mixing with the brown twigs and fir needles. Almost in the selfsame second a big gray lynx burst from the green of the underbrush and sprang upon the little, sprawling, helpless form.

But not actually upon it. Those outstretching, murderous claws never actually sank into the Kid's flesh. For Sonny was there just as soon as the lynx was. The wild beast changed its mind, and attack, just in time to avoid being taken at a serious disadvantage. The rush of Sonny's heavy body bore it backward clear of the Kid. The latter scrambled to his feet, stifled his sobs, and stared open-mouthed at the sudden fury of battle which confronted him.

Had Sonny not been endowed with intelligence as well as valour, he would have fallen victim almost at once to his adversary's terrific, raking hind claws. But fortunately, during his pugnacious puppyhood he had had several encounters with war-wise, veteran cats. To him, the lynx was obviously a huge and particularly savage cat. He knew the deadly power of its hind claws, with all the strength of those great hind quarters behind them. As he grappled with the screeching lynx, silently, after the fashion of his bull ancestors, he received a ripping slash from one of its armed fore paws, but succeeded in fixing his grip on the base of the beast's neck, not far from the throat. Instantly he drew himself backward with all his weight, crouching flat, and dragging the enemy down with him.

In this position, Sonny, backing and pulling with all his strength, the spitting and screeching cat was unable to bring its terrible hinder claws into play. The claws of the beast's great fore paws, however, were doing cruel work on Sonny's back and sides; while its long fangs, pointed like daggers, tore savagely at the one point on his shoulder which they could reach. This terrible punishment Sonny took stoically, caring only to protect the tender under part of his body and his eyes. His close grip on the base of the animal's neck shielded his eyes, and, according to the custom of his tenacious breed, he never relaxed his hold for a moment, but kept chewing in, chewing in, inexorably working his way to a final, fatal grip upon the throat. And not for a moment, either, did he desist from his steady backward pull, which kept the foe from doubling upon him with its hind quarters.

For several minutes the furious struggle went on, Sonny, apparently, getting all the worst of it. His back and shoulders were pouring blood; while his enemy showed not a hurt. Then suddenly the gray beast's screeching took on a half strangling sound. With its mouth wide open it ceased to bite, though its fore paws raked and clawed more desperately than ever. Sonny's relentless hold was beginning to throttle. His mouth was now too full of long fur and loose skin for him to bite clean through the throat and finish the fight. But he felt himself already the victor.

Suddenly, as he continued that steady backward drag, the resistance ceased.

The lynx had launched itself forward in one last convulsive struggle to free itself from those strangling teeth at its throat. For a second or two Sonny felt himself overwhelmed, engulfed, in a vortex of rending claws. In a tight ball of hate and ferocity and horror the two rolled over and over in the underbrush. Sonny, doubled up hard to protect his belly, heard a shrill cry of fear from the Kid. At the sound he summoned into his strained nerves and muscles a strength beyond the utmost which he had yet been able to put forth. His jaws worked upward, secured a cleaner grip, ground slowly closer; and at last his teeth crunched together. A great shudder shook the body of the lynx. It straightened out, limp and harmless.

For perhaps a minute Sonny maintained his triumphant grip, shaking the foe savagely. Satisfied, at last, that he was meeting with no more resistance, he let go, stood off, and eyed the body with searching suspicion. Then he turned to the Kid. The Kid, careless of the blood and wounds, kissed him fervently on the nose, called him "Poor Sonny! Dear, good Sonny!" and burst into a loud wailing.

Knowing that the one thing now was to get the Kid home again as soon as possible, Sonny started, looking back, and uttering a little imperative bark. The Kid understood, and followed promptly. By the time they reached the fence, however, Sonny was so weak from loss of blood he could hardly climb through. The Kid, with blundering but loving efforts, helped him. Then he lay down.

At this moment the voices of Joe and Ann were heard, shouting, calling wildly, from the yard. At the sound, Sonny struggled to his feet and staggered on, the Kid keeping close beside him. But he could manage only a few steps. Then he sank down again.

The man and woman came running up the pasture, calling the Kid; but the latter would not leave Sonny. He trotted forward a few steps, and stopped, shaking his head and looking back. When Joe and Ann came near enough to see that the little one's face and hair and clothes were splotched with blood, fear clutched at their hearts. "My God! what's happened to him?" gasped Ann, striving to keep up with her husband's pace. But Joe was too quick for her. Darting ahead, he seized the little one, lifted him up, and searched his face with frantic eyes. For all the blood, the child seemed well and vigorous.

"What's it mean, Kid? Ye ain't hurt--ye ain't hurt--tell me ye ain't hurt, Kid! What's all this blood all over ye?" he demanded breathlessly.

By this time Ann was at his side, questioning with terrified eyes.

"Tain't me, Unc' Joe!" protested the Kid. "I ain't hurted. It's poor Sonny. He's hurted awful. He killed the great, big--great, big--" the Kid was at a loss how to explain, "the great, big, dreadful cat, what was goin' to eat me up, Sonny did."

Joe Barnes looked at the dog, the torn sides, streaming red wounds, and bloody muzzle. Woodsman that he was, he understood. "Sonny!" he cried in a piercing voice. The dog raised his head, wagged his stump of a tail feebly, and made a futile effort to rise.

Gulping down something in his throat, Joe Barnes handed the child over to Ann, and strode to Sonny's side. Bending over him, he tenderly gathered the big dog into his arms, holding him like a baby. Sonny reached up and licked his chin. Joe turned and hastened back to the old gray house with his burden.

"Come along, mother," he said, his voice a little unsteady. "You'll have to look out for the Kid all by yerself for a bit now. I reckon I'm goin' to hev' about all I kin do, a-nursin' Sonny."

THE END